A study of the life and times of the Early Church,
as it relates to
the daily life of the modern Christian.

THE CHRISTIAN LIFE in the Early Church and TODAY

according to
St. Paul's SECOND Epistle
to the
Corinthians

By the same author:

THE CHRISTIAN LIFE in the Early Church and TODAY
according to
St. Paul's FIRST Epistle to the Corinthians

ARE YOU SAVED?
The Orthodox Christian Process of Salvation
(Fourth, Expanded Edition, 1997)

Cover Design by James P. Chicouris

THE CHRISTIAN LIFE
in the Early Church and TODAY

according to
St. Paul's SECOND Epistle
to the
Corinthians

by
BARBARA PAPPAS

Foreword by
BISHOP KALLISTOS OF DIOKLEIA
(Timothy Ware)

Amnos Publications
Westchester, Illinois

Library of Congress Cataloging-in-Publication Data

Pappas, Barbara, 1941-
The Christian life in the early Church and today : according to St. Paul's Second Epistle to the Corinthians / Barbara Pappas; with foreword by Timothy Ware. p. cm.
Includes bibliographical references and index.
ISBN 0-9623721-5-3 (pbk.)
1. Bible. N.T. Corinthians, 2nd—Criticism, interpretation, etc. 2. Christian life—Biblical teaching. 3. Christian life—Orthodox Eastern authors. I. Title.
BS2675.6.C48P372 1996
227' .306—dc20 96-18301
CIP

Amnos Publications
2501 South Wolf Road
Westchester, Illinois 60154
(708) 562-2744

to
George, John, Mike
sons of the Heart

Foreword

When we study Holy Scripture, so we are told by the Early Fathers, we should give a personal application to everything we read. Each of us should regard the words as addressed to me, myself, and not to someone else. We should ask not merely, "What does it mean?," but, "What does it mean *for me*, here and now?" The message of Scripture is to become an integral part of our daily life. "In everything that you do or say," St. Anthony of Egypt tells us, "take always as your guide the witness of the Holy Scriptures."

This is exactly what Barbara Pappas helps us to do, in this very welcome introduction to St. Paul's *Second* Epistle to the Corinthians. As in her previous book on the First Epistle to the Corinthians, she seeks to relate the words of the Bible to our present-day concerns. She is faithful to the Orthodox principle that our understanding of Scripture should be Patristic, and so at every point she quotes the Fathers, especially St. John Chrysostom, who more than any other author has shaped the "Scriptural mind" of Orthodoxy. But at the same time, she indicates the practical relevance of Scripture to every one of us at this present moment; she makes Paul and Chrysostom speak to us as our contemporaries. With good reason she calls her work *THE CHRISTIAN LIFE in the Early Church and TODAY*. Her words are simple but not superficial, and in her sections on "Food for Thought," she poses searching questions. All of this makes her book suitable for use equally by individuals and by study circles.

For many of us, I suspect, the Second Epistle to the Corinthians is not our favorite epistle. Probably we quote far more often from the First Epistle, with its precious references to the Eucharist (1Cor 10:16-17; 11:23-29), its image of the Church as a single body formed from many members united in love (12:12-13:13), and its vision of the final resurrection (15:12-58). By contrast, when reading the Second Epistle to the Corinthians we may easily grow restless when Paul insists at such length on the importance of fund-raising (chapters 8-9), while his repeated warnings and rebukes in the final section (chapters 10-13) may leave us discouraged. Yet, it would be greatly to our loss if, on these grounds, we were to neglect the Second Epistle, for it contains some of the Apostle's deepest teaching. In any case, is not Paul's insistence on almsgiving and mutual responsibility as timely today as ever it was in the past, and should not his warnings lead each of us to examine our own conscience?

For myself, I treasure the Second Epistle to the Corinthians more particularly because of four "great moments" which it contains:

First, there is the Trinitarian blessing with which Paul's letter concludes: *The grace of the Lord Jesus Christ, and the love of God, and the communion of the Holy Spirit be with you all* (13:14). This, along with the baptismal command at the end of St. Matthew's Gospel (28:19), is the most definite and explicit affirmation of the doctrine of the Trinity in the whole of the New Testament.

Second, the Epistle includes one of Paul's clearest statements about our salvation in Christ: *God was in Christ reconciling the world to Himself (5:19)*. Christ Jesus is our Savior, our "reconciler," because He is one with God the Father: He is the second person of the Holy Trinity, "true God from true God."

Third, Paul indicates not only *that* Christ saves us but also *how* He does so: He who is true God reconciles us to the Father by sharing totally in our humanness. *For you know the grace of our Lord Jesus Christ, that though He was rich, yet for your sakes He became poor, that you through His poverty might become rich* (8:9). It is typical of Paul that, in the middle of a passage of practical advice concerned with almsgiving, he includes—almost in passing—a concise phrase that sums up the whole meaning of the Incarnation. The "riches" of Christ are His divine glory; His "poverty" signifies His total solidarity with us in our alienated and fallen condition. There is a two-way exchange: Christ shares in our "poverty" and we in His "riches."

Fourth, in memorable words Paul sets before us our future hope, which is nothing less than an unending transfiguration and *Theosis* (deification): *But we all, with unveiled face, beholding as in a mirror the glory of the Lord, are being transformed into the same image from glory to glory* (3:18). "From glory to glory," says the Apostle: there is no limit or final end to our journey through eternity, for however great the "glory" to which we have attained, there is always a greater glory that still awaits us.

These four texts from the Second Epistle to the Corinthians have for many years helped me to set my compass as I pursue the spiritual journey. Other readers, with the help of this book, will discover their own personal guidelines or "great moments" in the Epistle.

"Christ is not a text but a living Person," says Father Georges Florovsky; and he also states that none of us will profit from reading Scripture unless at the same time we are "in love with Christ." May Barbara's book help us, as we study Scripture, to discover in and through the text the living Person of our Lord. May her words make us more "in love with Christ."

+BISHOP KALLISTOS OF DIOKLEIA

Acknowledgements

Words do not suffice to convey my gratitude to Bishop Kallistos of Diokleia. True shepherd and teacher that he is, his words in the Foreword add a dimension far beyond my own.

As always, Rev. William Chiganos offered invaluable leadership and support. Perry Hamalis, Connie Kappas, Carolyn Skoirchet and Nola Vandarakis offered constructive criticism, each from their own unique perspective. Linda Hardy and Ann Lampros offered not only valued insight but technical assistance as well. Each of these co-workers in our Lord's vineyard has left an imprint on the finished product. My gratitude is exceeded only by my high regard for their friendship.

Contents

Paul of Tarsus

(circa 3–67 A.D.)

Introduction

This work is a commentary on the Second Epistle to the Corinthians, fleshed out to include the many aspects of the Christian life touched-upon by St. Paul's letter. Based primarily on the Homilies of St. John Chrysostom, it focuses on Paul's advice to his spiritual children in Corinth rather than on dates and historical details. Chrysostom's guidance is priceless. Readers will find his words just as beneficial today as when they were written in the fourth century. Excerpts from his writings and those of many other Church Fathers are sprinkled liberally throughout the text because they vividly convey Orthodox theology with ageless clarity and beauty. Where appropriate, excerpts from contemporary authorities have been included to develop a modern tool, useful for teaching in the Church of today, the fullness of the truth of Scripture as lived and taught by the early Church...for God's word is never out of date.

Aspects of St. Paul's relationship with the Christians of Corinth have become the subject of modern contention (the dates of his visits, the number of letters he wrote to them, and the order in which they received his various letters). This study presumes the following traditional viewpoint:

The date of Paul's initial visit to Corinth is unknown. He followed-up on that visit with a letter (referred to in 1 Cor 5:9) which has been lost. Returning around 50 A.D., he remained eighteen months to establish a church there. Then he went to Ephesus, where he was visited by a delegation from Corinth, sent to apprise him of the problems that had developed in the community after his departure (1 Cor 7:1, 16:17). His response was a letter to his errant charges that has become known as his First Epistle to the Corinthians. Soon after, he sent Timothy to give them additional guidance (1 Cor 4:17). Timothy returned to Paul (1 Cor 16:11) and informed him that the spiritual situation was still not good in Corinth. Paul gave the Corinthians more time, then sent Titus to see how they were doing. Titus met up with Paul again in Macedonia. He brought the good news that, although the

Corinthians had at first resented the harsh words of his epistle, their hearts had softened as they realized his and Christ's love for them. They were now repentant and eager to see Paul again (2 Cor 7:6-9). Paul then wrote what we know as his *Second Epistle to the Corinthians* (c. 56 A.D.) to tell them he had not yet returned as promised because he did not want to be among them until they corrected their ways (2 Cor 1:23). Now, however, he hoped to come soon. He sent Titus back to Corinth with his latest letter (2 Cor 8:16-24, 9:1-5) to guide them in the merits of almsgiving and to be sure their collection for the church in Jerusalem would be ready when he arrived—his third visit.

Quotes from works of the following Church Fathers help to shed light on the issues raised by Paul's epistle (dates are approximate).

Andrew, Archbishop of Caesarea (c.600 A.D.)

Aphraates (280-345)

Athanasius, Bishop of Alexandria (c.298-373)

Augustine, Bishop of Hippo (354-430)

Basil, the Great, Archbishop of Caesarea (330-379)

Cassian, John (360-435)

Chrysostom, John (347-407)

Clement, of Alexandria (150-215)

Clement, Apostolic Father, Bishop of Rome (c.30-101)

Climacus, John (570-649)

Cyril, Patriarch of Alexandria (373-444)

Cyril, Patriarch of Jerusalem (318-386)

Cyprian, Martyr, Bishop of Carthage (200-258)

Ephraem, the Syrian (306-373)

Gregory, the Great, Bishop of Rome (540-603)

Gregory, the Theologian (of Nazianzus), Patriarch of Constantinople (329-390)

Gregory, of Nyssa (332-394)

Gregory, Palamas (1296-1359)

Ignatius, (second) Bishop of Antioch from 69 A.D.

Irenaeus, Martyr, (second) Bishop of Lyons from 178 A.D.

Justin, Martyr, Apostolic Father (100-165)

Leo, the Great, Bishop of Rome (440-461)

Makarios, of Egypt, the Great (300-390)

Mathetes—the title (meaning disciple) used by the anonymous author of the *Epistle to Diognetus*, who probably wrote toward the close of the apostolic age.[1]

Maximus, the Confessor (580-662)

Peter, of Damaskos (12th Century)

Philotheos, of Sinai (9th to 10th Century)

Polycarp, Martyr, Bishop of Smyrna (69-155), disciple of the Apostle John the Beloved

Sources have been cited exactly, except for minor updating of language. Words in brackets were added by the author for clarification. "Food for Thought" questions are included at appropriate points within the text, with comments on these questions at the end of each chapter. Scripture quoted is from the *New King James Version of the Holy Bible*. For the most productive use of this material, all referenced Scripture should be included in the reading.

[1] Alexander Roberts and James Donaldson, "Introductory Note to the Epistle of Mathetes to Diognetus," *THE ANTE-NICENE FATHERS, Translations of the Writings of the Fathers down to A.D. 325*, Vol. I, p.23.

CHAPTER ONE
Comfort in the Midst of Tribulation

BACKGROUND: Paul's epistles to the Corinthians served the early Church as a guide to the Christian life. They play the same role for us. The first epistle covers basics such as the need for love, fellowship, and unity in Christ in the Church; God's plan for our salvation through the Cross; Christian morality; the Church's views on marriage and celibacy; male and female roles; the gifts of the Holy Spirit; the importance of order in worship; the Mystery of the Eucharist and our participation in it; and the promised resurrection of the dead. This second epistle delves more deeply into spiritual matters such as growth in holiness, the role suffering plays in the Christian life, the need for almsgiving and prayer, the power of repentance and forgiveness, that which happens after death, the types of bodies the righteous and the unrighteous will have after the Resurrection, and the conditions of life in Heaven. In this letter Paul also bares his heart and soul. He has experienced the extremes of emotion, from the deep despair of unrelenting persecution and isolation to the ecstasy of being in the presence of God. His long, personal association with the Christians of Corinth allows him to share his disappointments and fears as well as his joys.

1:1. Paul, an apostle of Jesus Christ by the will of God, and Timothy our brother, to the Church of God which is at Corinth, with all the saints who are in all Achaia: Paul begins this epistle in a way which is common for him, by alluding to having literally been called by God to be an Apostle (Acts 9:1-22). This fact is especially important in this instance because there were those in Corinth who questioned his authority to teach the Gospel of Jesus Christ. Timothy, his spiritual son and co-worker, had visited the Corinthians as promised to reinforce Paul's work with them (1 Cor 4:17) and is now back in Macedonia with Paul.

Achaia was a Roman province covering that part of ancient Greece which was south of Thessaly and Macedonia; Corinth was its capital. However, all of Greece was often designated broadly as

Achaia. Paul's First Epistle to the Corinthians contained truths they specifically needed to be reminded of or to have clarified. In this Second Epistle, he addresses not only the Christians in Corinth but also those in all Achaia because he felt that they too were in need of counsel. His reference to a broader audience than the direct recipients of this letter indicates his awareness that these writings would be shared.

1:2. Grace to you and peace from God our Father and the Lord Jesus Christ. To receive *grace* is to partake of the energies of God (a bit of the power of the Creator) for the purpose of sanctification. We were created for fellowship with God (Acts 17:26-28). God is Holy, so to fulfill our potential we must become holy. But we cannot do so solely by our own efforts, only with God's grace. *Peace from God* is the inner state of contentment experienced by those who address their "reason for being" by cooperating with grace to make growth in holiness, in Christ's image, the focal point of their lives. If there is no grace in our lives, there can be no peace.

> Peace is serenity of mind, tranquility of soul, simplicity of heart, the bond of love, the fellowship of charity. It takes away enmities, restrains wars, holds back anger, treads down pride, loves the humble, calms those who quarrel, reconciles those who are enemies and is pleasing and acceptable to all. It seeks nothing that belongs to another; regards nothing as its own. It teaches a love that has never learned to hate. It knows not how to be lifted above itself. It knows not how to be puffed up.
>
> He who acquires this peace should hold fast to it. He who has broken it should strive to restore it. He who has lost it should seek earnestly to find it again. For whoever is found without this peace is rejected by the Father, disinherited by the Son and becomes a stranger to the Holy Spirit...He who is deliberately at enmity with another Christian cannot have the friendship of Christ.
>
> AUGUSTINE[1]

FOOD FOR THOUGHT: (a). To whom does God grant grace? Do we play a role in this matter, or are we subject to His whim as to whom He will give this gift and to whom He will not? (b). In the events of life, does God first give the grace that enables righteous action, or does He wait for righteous action first, then grant grace to strengthen our efforts?

1:3-4. Blessed be the God and Father of our Lord Jesus Christ, the Father of mercies and God of all comfort, Who comforts us in all our tribulation, that we may be able to comfort those who are in any trouble, with the comfort with which we ourselves are comforted by God. Jesus Christ brought the world the good news of life after death in God's eternal Kingdom for those who love Him. He was persecuted, scourged, and then crucified because the world did not want to hear His message. Now, about a quarter of a century later, Paul is following a similar path. He expresses his adoration of God, Who comforts him during these times of tribulation. With the understanding that...*all things work together for good to those who love God (Rom 8:28),* Paul affirms from experience that those who, during very difficult times, have felt the comfort that only God can provide, can in turn help bring that comfort to others.

FOOD FOR THOUGHT: (c). Why did the world not want to hear the message that Jesus brought? Why does the world still not want to listen? (d). Why does a loving God allow troubled times to enter the lives of His people?

1:5. For as the sufferings of Christ abound in us, so our consolation also abounds through Christ. Because Paul imitates Christ in his willingness to suffer in order that God's work may be done, he receives divine comfort. No amount of suffering is beyond the realm of this consolation. In the midst of agony, he who keeps his focus on God feels enveloped by His warm Presence. This gift cushions the harsh jolts of life and at the same time transforms the sufferer, rendering him able to endure the unendurable. With this gift, Stephen withstood, even joyfully, the blows of the stones cast at him by those who opposed the Gospel (Acts 7:55-60). Just as there would have been no Resurrection without the Cross, this type of comfort comes only as the companion of righteous suffering.

> Nothing can be harder to bear than bodily pain; nevertheless, because of this joy in God, what even to hear of is intolerable becomes both tolerable and longed for; and if you take the martyr from the cross or the gridiron barely still breathing, you will find a treasure of joy within him that words cannot describe.
>
> CHRYSOSTOM[2]

1:6. Now if we are afflicted, it is for your consolation and salvation, which is effective for enduring the same sufferings which we also suffer. Or if we are comforted, it is for your consolation and salvation. The Gospel is especially powerful when its teachers are not only willing to endure the tribulation their work inevitably brings, which proves their faith in its message of salvation, but when they also seem to possess deep inner joy in spite of troubled times. Those witnessing this demonstrated faith, love and power are consoled, strengthened, and encouraged to believe and live by God's word—so the cycle continues.

The subject of suffering stirs deep emotions. No one relishes the agony of physical or emotional pain. It is natural, alas human, to want to avoid situations with that potential. It is supernatural—touching upon the divine—to willingly endure voluntary suffering (like persecution or deprivation) in order that God's purposes be served, or to endure involuntary suffering (like severe illness or loss) without becoming bitter about life and toward God. Dealing with the troubled times of life can leave us bitter or better—the choice is ours.

1:7. And our hope for you is steadfast because we know that as you are partakers of the sufferings, so also you will partake of the consolation. Paul hopes that the Christians in Corinth will emulate his example and not shy away from the difficulties that living by and teaching the Gospel bring. His desire is not that they should suffer but that they partake of the fruit that comes from willingness to endure suffering when necessary, in order that Christ's work be done (see Rom 8:16-18 and Chapter 12 of this study).

> For no one who is self-indulgent has fellowship with Christ...nor anyone lax, lazy, indifferent or loose in behavior and morals. He who is in affliction and temptation and who is journeying on the narrow way is near to Him...so do not grieve when you are in affliction, considering with Whom you have fellowship, how you are purified by trials, and how great is your gain...Neither afflictions nor conspiracies, nor any other thing has power to grieve the right-minded soul. CHRYSOSTOM[3]

1:8. For we do not want you to be ignorant, brethren, of our trouble which came to us in Asia: that we were burdened beyond measure, above strength, so that we despaired even of life. In the course of his ministry in Ephesus, Paul faced many adversaries (1 Cor 16:8-9) and his life had been in great danger (Acts 19:21-30).

1:9. Yes, we had the sentence of death in ourselves, that we should not trust in ourselves but in God Who raises the dead... God allowed Paul to face the ever-present danger of death so he would learn that some things were beyond his control. Only when we have exhausted all of the world's means of dealing with a serious problem can we begin to understand that ultimately we can rely only on God for those things in life that really matter. When such events seem to be leading to a certain inevitable conclusion, then suddenly, after fervent prayer, they take a favorable turn against all odds—God's existence and power are demonstrated.

> When enemies devise mischief, God allows it to come even to the trial, and then works miracles; as in the case of the furnace and the lions (Dan 3:25). CHRYSOSTOM[4]

1:10. Who delivered us from so great a death, and does deliver us; in Whom we trust that He will still deliver us... In Ephesus, God shielded Paul from death by the hands of his enemies. He is confident that this deliverance will continue through future trials so he can continue his work.

When facing adversity, our first step is to turn to God in prayer and in Scripture, seeking His guidance, assistance, and strength.

If we then take the actions that seem best under the circumstances and trust God by leaving the rest to Him, that which will surface, endure, and triumph is our love for God and His for us (Mt 3:12)—no matter the outcome of the immediate situation.

God is in control. He has ultimate power over everything, including death. He created man to live forever. Thus, a form of life—of the soul—continues beyond the death of the body. In accordance with His divine plan, at the Second Coming of Christ, all who died believing in Him as Messiah will rise from their graves, with new bodies, and will inherit an eternal life of blessedness (I Thess 4:13-18). God constantly reassures us of this truth with signs of resurrection all around us: the new life of spring which follows the deadness of winter in the cycle of the seasons, the daily routine of activity followed by sleep then reawakening, and the various crises of life.

> When God lifts up again a man who is despaired of...He demonstrates a resurrection, snatching out of the very jaws of death him who had fallen into them: so in the case of those restored either out of grievous sickness or insupportable trials, it is natural to say, "We have seen a resurrection of the dead." CHRYSOSTOM[5]

***1:11. you also helping together in prayer for us, that thanks may be given by many persons on our behalf for the gift granted to us through many*.** While clearly attributing his deliverance from danger to God's mercy (vs 10), Paul emphasizes that this mercy is granted in response to prayer, private and corporate.

> We can pray in our own home; but it is not possible to pray there as in church, where the number is large and where prayer is offered up with one accord. When you pray alone your prayers are not heard in the same way as when you pray with your brethren. In the church there is something greater; the prayers are of one mind and one voice; there is the bond of charity and the prayer of the priests. It is for this reason the priests are there, so that joining their more efficacious prayers to those less strong of the people, they may ascend together with

> them to Heaven. For if the prayer of the Church helped Peter and delivered him from prison [Acts 12:5], how can you ignore its power. CHRYSOSTOM[6]

Jesus often illustrated the fact that God responds to prayer. He mercifully healed the daughter of the woman of Canaan after *she came and worshiped Him*, saying, *"Lord, help me"* (Mt 15:21-28); and He responded to the centurion's plea to *speak the word only,* and his servant was healed from a distance (Mt 8:5-13).

Paul also reminds us to remember to thank God—even if His answer to our prayers differs from our desires. These occasions present opportunities to show our trust in Him.

> **FOOD FOR THOUGHT:** (e). We know that God, in His omniscience, knows even the number of hairs on the heads of His people (Mt 10:30) and does not need us to keep Him informed of situations on earth. Why then is there such Biblical emphasis on prayer for one another, which is echoed in the Divine Liturgy and in the life of the Church? Does God always answer prayer? Are our prayers for others always of assistance to them? (f). Do our prayers for those who are experiencing difficulties eliminate the need to offer practical physical or emotional assistance?

Chrysostom points out that if we expect God's mercy in our lives in answer to prayer, we must be "worthy." He cites as an example, the Ninevites, who were saved when *they turned from their evil way* (Jonah 3:10). No one is ever worthy in the sense that they are deserving of God's mercy, for *all have sinned, and fall short of the glory of God* (Rom 3:23). Rather, worthiness is the state of grace of those who continually repent and acknowledge their dependence on Christ as Savior. Sincere repentance includes effort to change, so the worthy are those who try always to live in obedience to Christ, and who, when they inevitably fall short of this goal, rise to try again. Those who make this struggle a way of life demonstrate true faith in and love for God—the criteria for salvation.

> For our prayers to be heard by God, they must first come from one who is worthy of receiving. Secondly, they should be made in accordance with the laws of God. Thirdly, they should be unceasing. Fourthly, it is required of us that we pray with earnestness and not in a worldly manner. Fifthly, that we join with Him in bringing them about by asking only for what is fitting and expedient for us.
> CHRYSOSTOM[7]

As we mature spiritually, our prayers will change. The things of the world will seem less urgent. We will spend more time in praise, thanksgiving, and worship, and our petitions will reflect the desire that God's will be done.

> Seek from God our King the things that are worthy of Him and...do not cease praying till you receive them...If a month goes by, or a year, or three years, or four, or many, do not give up praying till you receive what you ask for; but ask on in faith, and at the same time be steadfast in doing good. It often will happen that someone strives earnestly for chastity in his youth. Then pleasure begins to undermine his resolution, desires awaken his nature, he grows weak in prayer, wine overcomes his youth, modesty perishes, and he becomes another man. So we change because we have not stood firm against our passions with high courage of soul. It behooves us, therefore, to resist all things, yet we must also cry out to God, that He may bring us aid.
> BASIL[8]

If God does not seem to respond to our prayers, we should reflect upon our life, our spiritual condition, and those things we ask of Him. As we pray for guidance we may begin to understand that there is a reason He does not grant particular petitions. Paul prayed that he be freed from his *thorn in the flesh* only until he realized that this affliction made his ministry more effective (2 Cor 12:7-10).

1:12. For our boasting is this: the testimony of our conscience that we conducted ourselves in the world in simplicity and godly sincerity, not with fleshly wisdom but by the grace of God, and more abundantly toward you. Paul's life is dedicated to doing God's work. He finds comfort in the fact that the suffering he has been experiencing was not caused by any wrongdoing on his part. The consolation referred to in 2 Cor 1:3-7 is the divine comfort given to those whose lives demonstrate faith, whereas this verse points to the human comfort of a clear conscience. A wonderful sense of well being is enjoyed by those who can look back on life and see that God had been at work in their helplessness if they also know that they tried, aided by His grace, to follow His will.

> Seeing that Paul had said *God comforted us*, and *God delivered us,* and had ascribed all to His mercies and their prayers, lest he should thus make the hearer negligent, presuming on God's mercy only and the prayers of others, he shows that he had contributed a great deal himself...from the purity of his life. CHRYSOSTOM[9]

1:13-14. For we are not writing any other things to you than what you read or understand. Now I trust you will understand, even to the end (as also you have understood us in part), that we are your boast, as you also are ours, in the day of the Lord Jesus. Paul teaches only the word of God as he received it. Those who accept his message of salvation through Christ—and try to live by it—will be part of God's Kingdom because of their faith. They will always be grateful to Paul for introducing them to the Gospel. Paul, in turn, will rejoice over those who, by responding favorably, became the fruit of his faith.

1:15-16. And in this confidence I intended to come to you before, that you might have a second benefit—to pass by way of you to Macedonia, to come again from Macedonia to you, and be helped by you on my way to Judea. Because of the spiritual bond between them, Paul was anxious to spend more time with the Corinthians. Thus he had intended to stop by on his way to Macedonia as well as after leaving Macedonia on his way to Judea (1 Cor 16:5).

1:17. Therefore, when I was planning this, did I do it lightly? Or the things I plan, do I plan according to the flesh, that with me there should be Yes, Yes, and No, No? He did not follow through with his original plan. Is he therefore fickle as his detractors claim? Does he say one thing but then do that which suits his fancy when the time comes to keep his word?

1:18-20. But as God is faithful, our word to you was not Yes and No. For the Son of God, Jesus Christ, Who was preached among you by us—by me, Silvanus, and Timothy—was not Yes and No, but in Him was Yes. For all the promises of God in Him are Yes, and in Him Amen, to the glory of God through us. Paul's change of itinerary casts no reflection on God's promises—which are steadfast. Man has limited knowledge; he must continually reassess situations in life in order to try to make the right decisions. God sees the whole picture; His word to us remains forever true and valid.

1:21-22. Now He Who establishes us with you in Christ and has anointed us is God, Who also has sealed us and given us the Spirit in our hearts as a deposit. The Holy Trinity is at work in every true believer. According to God's divine plan, His beloved "man" becomes a part of the Body of Christ (the Church) through Baptism and remains so through a life of faith. Thus all true Christians are united *in Christ*. Through the anointing of Chrismation, we receive the seal of the gift of the Holy Spirit. The consecrated myrrh used in this Sacrament indelibly inscribes the "seal," the mark of authenticity borne by those who thus receive this indwelling Presence, which brings grace, peace (2 Cor 1:2), and guidance to those who submit themselves to God's will. The Holy Spirit acts through both of these Sacraments, evoking confidence and joy in believers, thus providing a *deposit* (Gr: the arravon): a glimpse of that which awaits in the fullness of the Kingdom. Thus the joys of the Kingdom begin in this life, when we come to the realization of the existence and love of God, and grow to the degree that faith and love prevail within us.

> Being the light of the divinity, grace cannot remain hidden or unnoticed; acting in man, changing his nature, entering into a more and more intimate union with him, the divine energies become increasingly perceptible, revealing to man the face of the living God, "the Kingdom of God present with power" (Mk 9:1). This divine experience, says Palamas, is given to each according to his measure and can be more or less profound, depending

on the worthiness of those who experience it. The full vision of the divinity having become perceptible in the uncreated light, in its deifying grace, is "the mystery of the eighth day"; it belongs to the future age. However, those who are worthy of it attain the sight of "the Kingdom of God come with power" in this life, as the three Apostles saw it on Mount Tabor.[10]

FOOD FOR THOUGHT: (g). Ever since the Holy Spirit descended upon the Apostles in the upper room in Jerusalem, giving them power to preach the Gospel of Jesus Christ to all nations (Acts 2), man has had access to His indwelling presence. But what was the role of the Holy Spirit in Old Testament times? Did He offer any assistance to man during that age? (h). Why did Jesus say He had to leave so the Holy Spirit could come (Jn 16:7)? Were Jesus and the Comforter unable to be in the world at the same time?

1:23. Moreover I call God as witness against my soul, that to spare you I came no more to Corinth. Those who cooperate with the indwelling presence of the Holy Spirit also grow in discernment. When Timothy returned to Paul after spending time with the Corinthians to help them understand what the Gospel required of them (1 Cor 4:17), he reported that there was still turmoil in the church there. At that point Paul had not yet returned to Corinth because of the delays and difficulties he had encountered in his ministry. After Timothy's report, however, Paul felt guided by the Holy Spirit to further delay his return until they had time to correct their ways so he would not have to be harsh with them upon his arrival. He had given his counsel. His next step was to draw back to allow the Holy Spirit to work in their hearts. In much the same way, a concerned parent or teacher might at times delay confrontation with his charges to allow them, of their own free will, to live up to what is expected of them. There are times to be aggressive and times to stand back a little to allow slow but willing growth rather than demand begrudging compliance.

> The mind is a wonderful thing, and therein we possess that which is in the image of the Creator...But the mind has two faculties: the one evil, that of the demons which draws us on to their own apostasy; and the divine and the good, which brings us to the likeness of God. When, therefore, the mind remains alone and unaided, it contemplates small things, commensurate with itself. When it yields to those who deceive it, it nullifies its proper judgment and is concerned with monstrous fancies. Then it considers wood to be no longer wood, but a god; then it looks on gold no longer as money, but as an object of worship. If, on the other hand, it assents to its diviner part and accepts the boons of the Spirit, then, so far as its nature admits, it becomes perceptive of the divine...the mind which is impregnated with the Godhead of the Spirit is capable of viewing great objects; it beholds the divine beauty, though only so far as grace imparts and its nature receives...If the mind has been injured by devils it will be guilty of idolatry or will be perverted to some other form of impiety. But if it has yielded to the aid of the Spirit, it will have understanding of the truth and will know God. BASIL[11]

1:24. Not that we have dominion over your faith, but are fellow workers for your joy; for by faith you stand. Paul cannot force their compliance to his guidance. As a teacher of the Gospel, he can only try to make them aware of the wonders of God's Kingdom and to awaken their desire to partake of them. Salvation comes through faith in Christ, which no one can impose on another. With the gift of free will, each of us responds to that which we learn about God. That response forms a relationship between Him and us. At the Second Coming of Christ, that relationship will be the basis for the manner in which we will spend eternity.

> For faith and godliness are allied to each other...he who believes in Him is godly, and he who is godly, believes more. ATHANASIUS[12]

FOOD FOR THOUGHT: (i). What tests of faith are we likely to face in the times in which we live?

CHAPTER ONE
Food for Thought Comments

1(a). To whom does God grant grace? Do we play a role in this matter, or are we subject to His whim as to whom He will give this gift and to whom He will not?

God desires that everyone be saved. Thus His grace is available to all. But He insists upon honoring our free will, the gift which enables growth in holiness in His image (which includes His freedom of will), so does not force His will or His grace on us.

> God placed Adam in Paradise...endowing him with free will, that good might be his of his own free choice, as it is His Who sowed the seeds of it. Adam was to tend the immortal trees; the divine purposes, the lesser ones as well as the greater ones; naked and unashamed, living a life of perfect simplicity, without clothing and without shelter; for it was fitting that the one who was first made should be like this. And He laid on him a law; as material on which to exercise his free will. This law was a commandment, decreeing the trees he might make use of, and the one he might not. And this was the tree of knowledge; not because it was from the beginning evil, or that it was forbidden out of envy...but good if partaken of in due time. To me this tree was contemplation, as I understand contemplation, safe only for those to attempt who have arrived at a more perfect manner of life, not good for the more simple souls, not for those yet strong in earthly appetites; just as solid food is not suited to those of tender age, who have need rather of milk.
>
> GREGORY OF NAZIANZUS[13]

Salvation is a synergistic process involving God and man. God offers grace toward salvation. Those who are receptive to this gift avail themselves of its power to the extent that they open themselves to it and use it (to try to live a life of obedience as proof or demonstration of faith and love).

> Jesus, the Sun of Justice, has arisen. The rays of this spiritual Sun spread out in all directions; and one indeed receives less grace, and another more; not that grace so gives itself, it is our own disposition that supplies the measure. For as the sun is one which gives light to the whole universe, and its ray is one, and its splendor, yet it does not shine with equal light upon all the world. Here is wondrous and abundant sunshine, here there is less. This house has little sunlight, this has it more abundantly; not because the sun gives more to this house and less to that but according to the windows which were opened to it by those who build the houses it has more room to enter and pours in accordingly. And since our thoughts and purposes are the windows of our soul, when you open wide your heart you receive a larger more generous, divine favour; when you narrow your soul, you can but receive a less abundant grace. Open wide and lay bare your heart and soul to God, that His splendour may enter into you. CHRYSOSTOM[14]

We need God's help, however, in all good things—even to begin to open ourselves to His grace. He is able to give this assistance without interfering with our free will because He has foreknowledge. He guides toward salvation (thus it can be said, "predestines," in a cooperative not an arbitrary sense) those whom He foreknows will love Him (Rom 8:29). In a similar manner, a parent will often know how each of his children will react in a given situation, though he does not cause or dictate their response. The parent's knowledge of his children is imperfect and incomplete, but still it can enable him to guide each child in the way most likely to bear fruit. God's foreknowledge of each of us is perfect and complete. It allows Him to assist us in ways that are powerful but that do not intrude upon our freedom. If, for instance, God foreknows that someone's heart will be softened toward Him if given a chance (Jer 1:5), He may place determining influences in that person's path at the crucial moment. This explains why often, in the midst of situations seemingly devoid of the presence of God, there may arise a person with an ardent love for Him.

> When a miracle occurs, may it cause you joy...God has put His finger there, sometimes to reward, sometimes to

> punish, sometimes to encourage His faithful people and sometimes to lead sinners into the way of salvation.[15]

There are those, however, who believe that God grants saving grace to and consequently saves only those whom He preselects arbitrarily, with no personal input from man. The Orthodox Church considers this a heresy. According to this theory of arbitrary predestination, all mankind is rightfully damned because of the sin of Adam and Eve, but God redeems and grants grace and salvation to whom He wills, the "elect," and man can do nothing toward his election. If this were so, it would mean that God also wills that some are predestined to sin and damnation. Would a merciful, just, and loving God condemn all mankind except those whom He chooses arbitrarily, with no consideration of the mind, heart and actions of each person? If Jesus is the Savior of all mankind (1 Jn 4:14), how can anyone be automatically excluded from God's mercy through no personal fault of his own? If God predestines some to Heaven and the rest to Hell, why did Paul write that we must *all appear before the judgment seat of Christ* (2 Cor 5:10)?

> God made man a free agent from the beginning, possessing his own power, even as he does his own soul, to obey the behests of God voluntarily, and not by compulsion of God. For there is no coercion with God, but a good will towards us is present with Him continually. Therefore, He gives good counsel to all. And in man, as well as in angels, He placed the power of choice, so that those who yielded obedience might justly possess what is good, given indeed by God, but preserved by themselves. On the other hand, they who have not obeyed shall, with justice, receive punishment: for God kindly bestowed on them what was good; but they themselves did not diligently keep it, nor deem it something precious, but poured contempt upon His super-eminent goodness. Rejecting therefore the good, and spewing it out, they shall all deservedly incur the just judgment of God...
>
> If some had been made bad by nature, and others good, the latter would not be deserving of praise for being good, nor would the former be reprehensible...But because man is possessed of free will from the beginning, and God

> is possessed of free will, in Whose likeness man was created, advice is always given to him to keep fast the good, which is done by obedience to God. IRENAEUS[16]

False teachings on this subject emerged in various forms throughout the history of Christianity but are found most pervasively in the Protestant Reformation teachings of John Calvin's "salvation by *grace alone*." This heresy is said to have its roots in the debate between Augustine, of the fifth century, and his contemporary, the British monk Pelagius.[17] Pelagius taught that the human will takes the determining initiative in the matter of salvation: that man is self-sufficient, with ability to use his free will (unassisted) to choose not to sin. Augustine protested that this concept grossly understated God's role. In refuting it, however, he went to the other extreme, overstating the role God chooses to play. Though Augustine affirmed that God gave man free will, he did not believe that God's grace, when directed upon man, could be resisted. So, he surmised, God must not desire that all be saved; if He did, according to Augustine, certainly they would be. Thus, in his zeal to insure proper appreciation of the divine role in the salvation of man, Augustine diminished the place of man's free will. Also, his stance did not take into account the awesome mystery that God, the Omnipotent, is willing to share power with mere man, and that He never overrides man's will. Augustine apparently thought this would assign weakness to God. It actually shows His strength. God remains in control, even though, for His own purposes, He allows limited power to man (and even to the Devil). As Paul wrote, *the weakness of God is stronger than men* (1 Cor 1:25).

> Personal beings constitute the peak of creation, since they can become God by free choice and grace. With them, the divine omnipotence raises up a radical "intervention," an integral newness: God creates beings who like Him can—let us recall the Divine Council of Genesis—decide and choose. But these beings can decide against God: is this not for Him the risk of destroying His creation? This risk, it is necessary to reply, must, paradoxically, register its presence at the very height of omnipotence. Creation, truly to "innovate," creates "the other," that is to say, a personal being capable of refusing

> Him Who created him. The peak of all-powerfulness is thus received as a powerlessness of God, as a divine risk. The person is the highest creation of God only because God gives it the possibility of love, therefore of refusal. God risks the eternal ruin of His highest creation precisely that it may be the highest. The paradox is irreducible: in his very greatness, which is to be able to become God, man is fallible; but without fallibility there would be no greatness. That is why, confirm the Fathers, man must undergo a test...so as to gain awareness of his freedom, of the free love that God awaits from him.[18]

God allowed theological contention such as this question of predestination in the early Church so His truths would surface from the ensuing debate (1 Cor 11:19). Pelagianism was condemned in 431 by the Third Ecumenical Council in Ephesus.[19] Augustine's teachings were tempered with the balance which has always been taught in the Orthodox Church—a wondrous cooperation of divine grace and human freedom.

Those referred to as God's "elect" or "chosen" are those who use their free will first to come to an understanding and acknowledgement that a divine Creator exists and then to fulfill the purpose for which they were given life: union with Him. Along every step of the way, however, man can do nothing without God's grace. God elects to grant grace to, and thus to save, those who open their hearts to Him, but He compels no one.

1(b). In the events of life, does God first grant grace, which enables righteous action and spiritual growth, or does He wait for righteous action first, then grant grace to strengthen our efforts?

Being omniscient, God knows not only the actions but also the mind and heart of man. He reaches out to us in many ways, as through the wonders of creation, and in every instance foreknows who will opt to follow the divine will rather than his own. He does not force His will upon us, however, because He wants us to choose freely to follow Him. At the very moment we lean toward God, even in thought, we open ourselves to divine grace, which strengthens us to the degree we allow. This divine power enables right action.

> The grace of God is not able to visit those who flee salvation. Nor is human virtue of such power as to be adequate of itself to raise up to authentic life those souls who are untouched by grace...But when righteousness of works and the grace of the Spirit come together at the same time in the same soul, together they are able to fill it with blessed life. GREGORY OF NYSSA[20]

Thus for short-term actions it is often harder to make a decision to act in accordance with God's will than it is to follow through with the subsequent action required. As the choice to act rightly is made (not before and not after), suddenly, through the grace of God, our vision is clearer, the burden seems lighter, and though the task may not be easy, God helps us keep our resolve. For long term actions the follow-through can be more difficult than the decision, but grace remains as strength and support as long as we choose to follow God's lead.

> The Lord's help is always there. Lest our free will should bring us to utter ruin, He is there, a hand stretched out to rescue and strengthen us when He sees us stumbling. CASSIAN[21]

1(c). Why did the world not want to hear the message that Jesus brought? Why does it still not want to listen?

The Gospel requires that we live according to God's will rather than our own. When Christ came to bring the good news of the Way to the Kingdom of Heaven, most Jews rejected Him because (being under Roman rule) they were looking for a Messiah who would free them from subjugation to others and create for them a kingdom on earth. Most pagans rejected Him because they did not want to exchange their many indulgent "gods" for a God Who demanded major changes in their lifestyles. In the modern world, many do not want to hear the Gospel for similar reasons: our society continues to lean toward self-will and instant gratification of desires. This accounts for the fact that *many are called, but few chosen* (Mt 20:16).

> The body has eyes to see creation...and recognize the Creator; ears to listen to the divine oracles and the laws

> of God; and hands both to perform works of necessity and to raise to God in prayer; yet the soul, departing from contemplation of what is good...wanders away and moves toward evil.... Instead of beholding creation, she turns the eye to lusts, showing that she has this power too; and thinking that by the mere fact of moving she is maintaining her own dignity and is committing no sin in doing as she pleases. She does not know that she is made not merely to move, but to move in the right direction.
>
> ATHANASIUS[22]

1(d). Why does a loving God allow troubled times to enter the lives of His people?

God allows (does not cause) His people to pass through the difficult times that life in our fallen world entails to test and strengthen their faith and love and to keep them on the right path. Many important lessons can be learned through adversity. He who turns to God in times of tribulation learns to persevere. Perseverance produces character; and character, hope (Rom 5:3-4), which comes ultimately only from the truth of Resurrection.

> ...the cold, ice, snow, frost, and violent winds... which plants withstand during the winter and summer, being exposed to the chill and heat...are the miseries without which nothing on earth can ever grow, being unable to reach fruition...These are the various difficulties which befall us, which every person who meditates on bearing the future fruit to be brought to the Spiritual Vinedresser must necessarily undergo with thanksgiving. For example, if one has mercy and protects the developing vegetation from miseries by building a wall around them and covering them with a roof so that they might withstand all the terrible seasonal weather conditions against them—and even takes special care of them by trimming and cleaning them—they will not bear fruit. Instead one must allow the plants to undergo all of this. For after the winter's unpleasantness, when springtime comes and blossoms, and leaf-bearing appears, together with that beautiful renewal of budding, the unripe fruit which then grows according to its little contact with the jutting rays of the sun ripens, produces and gives back pleasant food ready for harvesting.

> In the same way, a human being who does not endure courageously the unpleasant burdens of life will never produce fruit worthy of the divine wine-press and eternal harvest, not even if he possesses all other virtues.
>
> GREGORY PALAMAS[23]

Also, if life contained no hardships to endure or obstacles to overcome—if everything we dealt with day to day was without care—we would forget the purpose for life.

> We are afflicted in this life by the supremely good purpose of God, so that we may not love the way more than the end of our journey. For this present life is but a way by which we travel towards our heavenly home. And because of this we are, in the inscrutable wisdom of God, wearied by frequent disquiet, so that we may not come to love the way more than our home. For there are travelers who, when on their way, see some smiling field, and while they delight in its beauty, they slow their steps and turn aside from the straight path they had begun. The Lord therefore has made the way of this world hard for His Elect in their journey to Him, so that none of them may take his rest in this life, enjoying the beauty of the way, but may speedily hasten towards Him rather than linger by the way; or lest, delighting in the way, they come to forget they once longed for their heavenly home.
>
> GREGORY THE GREAT[24]

Yes, we should take time to "stop and smell the roses" when the opportunity presents itself. Brief respites refresh us physically and spiritually and give us strength to continue. Jesus often withdrew from the crowds for precisely these reasons (Lk 6:12; 8:22) but then got right back to the work He had been given to do.

Hear me when I call, O God of my righteousness! You have relieved me when I was in distress; Have mercy on me, and hear my prayer (Ps 4:1). Notice that the psalmist did not say "you have prevented me from falling into distress." God is certainly able to make our path through life free of care. He does not choose to do so, however, because that would not be to our best advantage. He does promise that we can count on Him to hear our prayers and to help us carry the particular cross life brings to us (Mt 10:38), but only if He sees, by the way we live, that we truly want to belong to Him and grow in union with Him. (For more on this topic, see 2 Cor 12:7-10.)

> It is not the hanging on a cross only that makes a Martyr, for were this so, then Job was excluded from this crown. He neither stood at bar, nor heard Judge's voice, nor looked on executioner, nor while hanging on tree aloft had his sides mangled; yet he suffered worse than many martyrs. More sharply than any stroke did the tale of those successive messengers strike and goad him on every side; and keener the gnawings of the worms which devoured him in every part than a thousand executioners.
>
> Against what martyr may he not worthily be compared? Surely against ten thousand. For in every kind of suffering he both wrestled and was crowned; in goods, and children, and person, and wife, and friends, and enemies and servants (for these too spit in his face), in hunger and visions and pains and noisomeness. And if any ask, "how can we bear these sufferings nobly?"...by one word of thanksgiving you shall gain more than all you have lost. For if at the tidings of our loss we be not troubled, but say, "Blessed be God," we have found far more abundant riches.
>
> CHRYSOSTOM[25]

The purpose for life is to choose whether we want to spend eternity with God in His Kingdom or away from Him, far removed from His blessings. We cannot avoid making this decision. Whether consciously or subconsciously, we make our choice and spend our lives demonstrating it, walking toward our eternal destination. If we choose to be with God, we must actively live that choice through a concerted attempt at obedience to the way of life He asks of His people, despite any adversity life may bring—the true test. The person who lives in this manner is guided and empowered by the Holy Spirit to the degree he allows, thereby producing, accordingly, the fruit of holiness, a state-of-being necessary for life in the Kingdom, where all is holy. Since nothing in life remains static, those who make the opposite choice or who neglect to make a choice—which amounts to the same thing (Mt 12:30)—continue to grow away from God. They set the eternal stage for themselves.

> According to St. Maximus, freedom of choice is already a flaw, a limitation of true freedom: perfect nature has no need of choice, for it knows what is good in a natural way. Its freedom is based on this knowledge. Our freedom of will reveals the imperfection of fallen human nature, the loss of God's likeness. Since this nature is obscured by sin, it does not know its true good and is directed constantly to what is "antinature." Thus the human person is always confronted by the necessity of choice. It gropes its way forward. This vacillation in the ascent to what is good is known as "freedom of will." The person, called to union with God, to perfect assimilation through grace of his nature with divine nature, is bound to a mutilated nature, crippled by sin, ravaged by contradictory desires. Knowing and willing according to this imperfect nature, the person is, in practice, blind and weak. It no longer knows how to choose and too often yields to the impulses of a nature which has become the slave of sin. In this way, what was made in us in God's image is drawn down into the abyss, although it still retains its freedom of choice and its ability to return to God.[26]

1(e). We know that God, in His omniscience, knows even the number of hairs on the heads of His people (Mt 10:30) and does not need us to keep Him informed of situations on earth. Why then is there such Biblical emphasis on prayer for one another, which is echoed in the Divine Liturgy and in the life of the Church? Does God always answer prayer? Are our prayers for others always of assistance to them?

The emphasis on praying for one another in Scripture and in the Church is not to keep God informed but to remind us to talk to Him regularly and to encourage us to be concerned about and to love one another (Jn 13:35, Jas 5:16). It is only by growing in this love and fellowship that we can begin to understand God's love for us and can grow in love for Him. Prayer is an important and powerful way to help in any situation. When someone is experiencing any difficulty, we can offer the comfort of a promise to pray for them—but then we must be sure to do so.

> The laws of the Church command prayer be made, not only for those in the Church but also those still outside...For when the Deacon says, "Let us pray earnestly for the catechumens," he encourages the faithful to pray for them; although they are not yet of the Body of Christ, they have not yet partaken of the Mysteries and are still divided from the spiritual flock.
>
> CHRYSOSTOM[27]

> We do it also because we desire to remain longer in His presence, attentively addressing yet more words to Him, giving thanks to Him, acknowledging the many blessings we have received from Him, for as long as we can.
>
> PETER OF DAMASKOS[28]

God always answers the sincere and fervent prayers of the righteous (Jas 5:16) but perhaps not always in the way expected or desired. His ultimate concern is for our spiritual welfare and salvation, whereas, too often our primary concerns are ease and pleasure in the world. Consequently, His guidance may not correspond with the direction in which our will leads.

Because God does not force His will on anyone, for the most part our prayers for others will bear fruit only if they are not blocking God out of their lives.

> What does this mean? Does prayer not help? It helps, and exceedingly, but only when we cooperate with it.
>
> ...But someone will say, "What need have I of the prayers of others, since I please God?" What are you saying? Paul did not say, "What need have I of prayers?" Peter did not say, "Why do I need prayers?" though those who prayed for him were not worthy of him, certainly they were not his equals. Yet you say: "What need have I of prayers?" You need them for this reason: because you think that you have no need them. CHRYSOSTOM[29]

1(f). Do our prayers for those who are experiencing difficulties in their lives eliminate the need to offer physical or emotional assistance?

Prayer should be our immediate and continual response to the difficult circumstances of life for those around us. In addition to our private and corporate prayers as part of the Church, however, God also expects us to be His co-workers in helping to meet the practical physical and emotional needs of those who are under duress. We can accomplish this by literally being the hands, feet, mouth and heart of Christ in doing what we can to help (1 Cor 3:9; 12:12,27-28). When there is a need, we can hold a frightened hand, shovel a driveway, drop-off groceries, scrub a floor, contribute financially, or do whatever is helpful. By doing so, we are being the Body of Christ. In trying to help we must remember that each situation is different, so it is important to use discernment. Sometimes it is best just to be around to show love and support and, when the opportunity presents itself, to bolster confidence in God's assurances that He loves us all and will help those who turn to Him in distress. At other times it may be best to stand back and wait for signs of when or how we may be helpful.

> Prayer is not made perfect by uttering syllables...but in the purpose of the soul and in the just actions of a lifetime.
> BASIL[30]

1(g). Ever since the Holy Spirit descended upon the Apostles in the upper room in Jerusalem, giving them power to preach the Gospel to all nations (Acts 2), man has had access to His indwelling presence. But what was the role of the Holy Spirit in Old Testament times? Did He offer any assistance to man during that age?

The Holy Spirit did not dwell within man until the day of Pentecost, after Jesus Christ ascended to His Father. The man of God of the Old Testament was not, however, completely denied the powerful presence of the Comforter. Since the time of Pentecost, God works within willing man; before then, He worked on man from the outside.

> The Old Testament did not know the intimate sanctification by grace, yet it knew saintliness, for grace, from outside, aroused it in the soul as an effect. The man who submitted to God in faith and lived in all righteousness could become the instrument of His will.

> As is proved by the vocation of prophets, it is not a question of agreement between two wills but of lordly utilization of the human will by that of God: the Spirit of God swoops upon the seer, God takes possession of man by imposing Himself from outside on his person. God, invisible, speaks: His servant listens.[31]

1(h). Why did Jesus say He had to leave so the Holy Spirit could come? Were Jesus and the Comforter unable to be in the world at the same time?

Jesus and the Holy Spirit can indeed be present in the world at the same time. In fact, the three persons of the Holy Trinity are never totally separated.

> God...the Cause, the Maker, the Perfecter, that is, the Father, the Son and the Holy Spirit...are not so separate from each other that they are divided in nature; and neither are they so confined in their nature as to be restricted to one Person. GREGORY OF NAZIANZUS[32]

Referring to the Holy Trinity, Jesus said: *If anyone loves me, he will keep My word, and My Father will love him, and* ***We*** *will come to him and make* ***Our*** *home with him* (Jn 14:23). Speaking of the Holy Spirit, Jesus said: *you know Him, for He dwells with you and will be in you* (Jn 14:17).

> From this we understand that God the Trinity dwells all together in the sanctified as in a temple. AUGUSTINE[33]

> In every operation the Spirit is closely joined with, and inseparable from, the Father and the Son. God works the differences of operations and the Lord the diversities of administrations, but all the while the Holy Spirit is present too of His own will, dispensing distribution of the gifts according to each recipient's worth. BASIL[34]

These truths are evident in the life of the Church (Orthopraxia). We wish each other God's presence when we say, "God be with you." We partake of the Body and Blood of Christ, and thus become one with Jesus continually, through Eucharist. We receive the indwelling of the Holy Spirit through the Sacrament of

Chrismation. Why then did Christ say that He had to depart so the Holy Spirit could come to be with man (Jn 16:7)?

> It appears to me that the disciples were taken up with the human figure of the Lord Christ, and, as men, were held by their human love for Him as a man. He began now to wish them to have rather a divine love and so change them from unspiritual men to spiritual: which a man does not become without the gift of the Holy Spirit. Therefore, this is what He says: I shall send you a gift whereby you will become spiritual men; namely, the gift of the Holy Spirit. But you cannot become spiritual men unless you cease to be unspiritual. You will cease to be unspiritual if this human form is taken from before your eyes. AUGUSTINE[35]

Jesus Christ promised to be with His people always (Jn 6:56, Mt 28:20) and is, via the Church through Eucharist. He left them bodily, however, to turn their attention to the Holy Spirit so they could begin to understand spiritual growth in holiness.

1(i). What tests of faith are we likely to face in the times in which we live?

A Christian faces many tests of faith during his lifetime. Decisions must continually be made on such issues as friends, career, spouse, moral and ethical questions and the like. Our ultimate decisions will indicate whether we are guided by faith in and love for God and His Son or by other factors. Whatever comes first in our hearts is "god" to us. The telling factor is whether we recognize the Creator as our Master and put obedience to Him first in our lives, or whether something else, such as money, fame, power, position, pleasure or acquisitions dominate and, therefore, take His rightful place. Nothing—not even family—should take precedence over God. If we put Him first and act accordingly, everything else will be in proper perspective (Mt 6:33). To attend to the reasonable needs of our family is to do God's work. If we have concern for our own soul and the souls of others but fail to try to nurture spiritually those who are closest to us, we are *worse than unbelievers* (1 Tim 5:8). But when our primary allegiance is to God, His grace makes us capable of ever more meaningful relationships with our loved ones. There will always be many demands upon the limited time, talent and resources we have at our disposal. Discernment must be used to establish priorities. The effort we expend to learn and to live by the precepts of God's divine plan, rather than fall to the temptation to make our own rules with regard to contemporary issues, sexual conduct, achieving success, etc., will bear much fruit in our lives.

> We ask not to have sound judgment and virtuous deportment for one day only, or for two or three, but through the whole tenor and period of our life; and as the foundation of all good things, to seek not our own, but *the things which are of Christ Jesus* (Phil 2:21). How might this be? (For besides prayer, it is necessary that we contribute also our own endeavors.) We must be occupied in His law *day and night*...[Josh 1:8, Ps 1:1-2, Acts 26:7, Rev 7:15.]
>
> I blush for those who are scarcely seen in Church once a year. For what excuse can they have who are bidden not simply *day and night* to commune with the law, but "to be occupied in it," that is, to be forever holding converse with it, and yet scarcely do so for the smallest fraction of their life? CHRYSOSTOM[36]

Serious illness and death are always tests of faith. When faced with them, those who want to be in God's Kingdom must resist the human tendency to become bitter and turn away from Him. Rather, it is important that during those times we pray for strength and guidance. When facing illness, we should pray for healing and for direction in seeking proper medical care; but if healing does not come, we should ultimately accept His will not to intervene as we ask and pray for strength to deal with the difficulties confronting us. In this instance, the fruit of prayer is acceptance and trust. We do not have to like a situation to accept it—and to accept a situation we do not like or understand is trust. If we do this, we are never alone in our difficulties—God is with us.

> It will happen even to steadfast courageous minds to be shaken by the fear of death. It is for this reason that some came to Christ praying: *Lord, increase our faith* (Lk 17:5). He who continues to offend through weakness of faith

falls short of the fullness of faith. For as gold is tested in fire, so is faith by temptation. But the mind of man is weak and needs help from above so that he may with courage face the dangers of the way. And this our Savior teaches when He says: *Without me you can do nothing* (Jn 15:5). And the most wise Paul confesses: *I can do all things in Him who strengthens me* (Phil 4:13).

CYRIL OF ALEXANDRIA[37]

CHAPTER TWO

On Being the Fragrance of Christ to God

BACKGROUND: Because of his deep affection for the Christians of Corinth, Paul had not yet returned to visit them as he had promised. In this chapter he explains this decision and addresses the claims of his detractors who were using his prolonged absence as an opportunity to claim that he was a false apostle.

2:1-2. But I determined this within myself, that I would not come again to you in sorrow. For if I make you sorrowful, then who is he who makes me glad but the one who is made sorrowful by me? If Paul had returned to visit the Corinthian Christians while the sinfulness he had written about in First Corinthians was still taking place, he would not have been able to hide his disappointment. His demeanor would have caused them sorrow. He loved them and wanted to be with them, but not under those circumstances.

2:3. And I wrote this very thing to you, lest, when I came, I should have sorrow over those from whom I ought to have joy, having confidence in you all that my joy is the joy of you all. He wrote in First Corinthians that their conduct would determine how he would next come to them—*with a rod, or in love and a spirit of gentleness* (1 Cor 4:21). He wanted to arrive joyfully, so they could share his joy.

2:4. For out of much affliction and anguish of heart I wrote to you, with many tears, not that you should be grieved, but that you might know the love which I have so abundantly for you. He had written in a stern tone admonishing them for their misconceptions and wrongdoings because he loved them and wanted the best for them—salvation. Yet his harshness had given him much pain, the type a parent feels when he must reprimand his children or punish their disobedience in order to keep them on the right path.

> A father whose...son is afflicted with gangrene, being compelled to use the knife and cautery, is pained on both accounts, that his son is diseased, and that he is compelled to use the knife on him. CHRYSOSTOM[1]

2:5. But if anyone has caused grief, he has not grieved me, but all of you to some extent—not to be too severe. The sinfulness in Corinth is not a personal affront to Paul but a matter which brings sorrow to the whole Church (see 1 Cor 12:26).

> **FOOD FOR THOUGHT:** (a). How can one person's sinfulness bring sorrow to the whole Church?

2:6-8. This punishment which was inflicted by the majority is sufficient for such a man, so that, on the contrary, you ought rather to forgive and comfort him, lest perhaps such a one be swallowed up with too much sorrow. Therefore I urge you to reaffirm your love to him. The man referred to had been involved in a sexual relationship with his stepmother (1 Cor 5:1). The action Paul insisted upon at the time was excommunication. He hoped that this would spark the offender's desire to return to the fellowship of the Church, thus encouraging him to repent and put an end to his sinful behavior. Apparently this spiritual discipline produced the desired results. The man involved must have shown repentance because Paul is now urging that they show love by taking the next step, which is to forgive him and welcome him back into their fellowship. Some of the Corinthians balked at this, prompting Paul's concern that the man involved will become discouraged—and be lost permanently.

> If one lets go him that has been scourged and heals him not, he has done nothing. CHRYSOSTOM[2]

> **FOOD FOR THOUGHT**: (b). How might a person be lost to the Church and to God's Kingdom through *too much sorrow*?

2:9. For to this end I also wrote, that I might put you to the test, whether you are obedient in all things. Paul's hope is that as they responded to the disciplinary action required they would now respond to the offender's repentance with forgiveness.

> Obedience to the stern measure of excommunication might seem to have stemmed from envy and malice, but subsequent forgiveness shows the obedience to be pure and whether they are prone to loving kindness...not because he is worthy, not because he has shown sufficient penitence, but because he is weak. CHRYSOSTOM[3]

In forgiving the excommunicated man and receiving him again into fellowship, the Corinthians would be demonstrating their faith and love. The penitent's faith and love are demonstrated by his repentance and desire to be reinstated, signifying his understanding of himself as a weak human being: unable to save himself and dependent upon the mercy and the grace of God through the saving actions of Jesus Christ. This is the proper work of the Church.

> The Church is...a court of justice, a hospital, a school of philosophy, a nursery of the soul, a training course for that race which leads to Heaven....and a spiritual bath which wipes away not filth of body but stains of soul, by its many methods of repentance. CHRYSOSTOM[4]

Excommunication was a tool used often in the early Church to safeguard the true teachings of Christ until they could be preserved by written dogma. The Mystery of Repentance/Confession and the authority to prescribe spiritual penance came to be understood in time as the vehicle by which the priest can lead his flock away from sin (Jn 20:23). The value of this instance of excommunication in Corinth is that it shows the zeal with which Paul taught the need for Christians to live in a Christ-like manner.

2:10-11. Now whom you forgive anything, I also forgive. For if indeed I have forgiven anything, I have forgiven that one for your sakes in the presence of Christ, lest Satan should take advantage of us; for we are not ignorant of his devices. Just as sin affects the whole Church, so do the appropriate corrective actions and subsequent forgiveness or lack thereof. True repentance should be responded to with the forgiveness that Christ taught, else the Body of Christ will be divided and Satan will win souls: those of the unforgiven, if they then stray from Christ, and the souls of those who refuse to forgive, through disobedience and hardness of heart. Those who withhold forgiveness from someone who has truly repented have no right to expect Christ's forgiveness for their sins (Mk 11:26).

> **FOOD FOR THOUGHT:** (c). What is true repentance? Must one continue forever in despair about past sins?

2:12-13. Furthermore, when I came to Troas to preach Christ's Gospel, and a door was opened to me by the Lord, I had no rest in my spirit because I did not find Titus my brother; but taking my leave of them, I departed for Macedonia. When Paul decided against returning to Corinth, he asked Titus to go instead and then to meet him in Troas to advise him on the progress the Corinthians were making in responding to the first epistle. When Paul arrived in Troas, however, he did not find Titus waiting for him. There was no means of instant communication to inquire about his whereabouts so Paul became anxious. Though there had been work for him to do in Troas, he left for Macedonia, hoping Titus would be there.

> **FOOD FOR THOUGHT:** (d). Think about the fact that even Paul experienced moments of despondency. What can we learn from his example (verse 2:14) in coping during difficult times in our lives?

2:14. Now thanks be to God Who always leads us in triumph in Christ, and through us diffuses the fragrance of His knowledge in every place. Paul had been in a poor state of mind. As a teacher of the Gospel, he had been enduring continual persecution. Although he longed to be in Corinth, he considered it the wrong time to return. In addition, he had been without the comfort and support of Titus when he needed it. In this verse, however, he joyously thanks God, Who not only brought him through this distressed state but in spite of it continued to use him as an instrument through which the glorious truths about Jesus Christ were dispersed wherever he went.

> We are Royal censers, breathing wherever we go of the heavenly ointment and the spiritual sweet savor.
> CHRYSOSTOM[5]

From the time God first began to point out the road to salvation to fallen man, the burning of incense to God has symbolized self-denying obedience. Aaron was commanded to burn incense perpetually (Ex 30:7-8). The constant, smoldering fragrance that ensued was a reminder of the sacrifices required by the Mosaic Law—the Old Testament Written Covenant between God and man. This created a *sweet aroma to the Lord* (Lev 2:2) because it indicated man's love for God. But the process was frustrating and futile because man could never keep up. The Law had to be followed exactly—legalistically. Each time a person disobeyed a segment of it, he was required to bring the prescribed atonement to the Temple. But he would inevitably disobey again, so found himself under continual bondage. Prefiguring the next step in God's divine plan for the salvation of mankind through the coming Messiah, the Psalmist groaned in desperation and asked that his prayers be likened to incense, rising to God with a sweet savor (Ps 141:2): that the intent of his heart be acknowledged and judged, rather than his incessant, external, legalistic attempts to follow the Law. Rev 5:8 and 8:3-4 confirm that, in response to that yearning, God sent His Son to usher in the new covenant. The blood Christ shed willingly for the redemption of mankind put an end to the legalistic sacrifices required under the Law. According to the terms of the new covenant, the prayers of all the *saints* rise before God as sweet smelling incense. "Saints" are those who attempt to live their lives in a manner which matches their prayers: trying to be Christ-like in all things to show love and faith in Christ as Savior but freed from the necessity to *achieve* absolute perfection to *earn* salvation.

> The odors of incense signify the fragrant sacrifice of the faithful which they offer by an undefiled life... The vials are thoughts from which come the fragrance of good deeds and pure prayer. ANDREW OF CAESAREA[6]

Malachi prophesied that the day would come when incense would be offered to God by Gentiles everywhere (Mal 1:11). In fulfillment of that prophecy, incense is a companion to prayer in the Orthodox Church. The lingering fragrance of incense is a reminder that, under the Blood Covenant of the New Testament, God's criterion for salvation is not a legalistic following of rules, but a life which is made sweet by faith in and love for Christ. God gave the Mosaic Law to the nation of Israel as a step toward learning obedience, and as an indication of what it would mean to be perfect and holy like Christ, Who *has loved us and given Himself for us, an offering and a sacrifice to God for a sweet-smelling aroma* (Eph 5:2).

> When our soul's own intrinsic qualities and fruits—prayer, love, faith, vigilance, fasting and the other expressions of the virtues—mingle and commune in the fellowship of the spirit, they effuse a rich perfume, like burning incense. MAKARIOS OF EGYPT[7]

2:15. For we are to God the fragrance of Christ among those who are being saved and among those who are perishing. The Gospel of Jesus Christ sets forth the terms by which all mankind may be saved from damnation (eternity in the everlasting torment of being away from the presence of God). Christ's life on earth, bringing this Gospel to mankind, created an aroma that pleased God. Those who continue Christ's work emit the same sweet aroma, discernible to God, whether the message they bring is accepted or rejected.

It is sobering to consider that if those who teach the good news of salvation through Jesus are *the fragrance of Christ* to God, those who defy the Gospel or ignore it (the same thing/Mt 12:30), must bear the odor of Satan.

> When the fear of God is not present with strictness, the soul is dead...It is not dissolved into corruption by ashes and dust, but into things of fouler odor than these: into drunkenness and anger and covetousness, into improper loves and unseasonable desires. If you want to know exactly how foul an odor it has, give me a soul that is pure, and then you will see clearly how foul the odor of this filthy and impure one...For so long as we are in contact habitually with a foul odor, we are not sensitive to it. CHRYSOSTOM[8]

FOOD FOR THOUGHT: (e). Have you asked yourself what type of aroma your life emits to God?

2:16. To the one we are the aroma of death to death, and to the other the aroma of life to life. And who is sufficient for these things? The Gospel is the same to all, but because of free will, each person receives it differently. Some hear and take it gladly into their hearts, choosing to take the road through life which leads to salvation. Others ignore or reject it, choosing instead the road to eternity away from God. To the one who accepts it, the Gospel carries the sweet aroma of eternal life. To the one who rejects it, its aroma is made caustic by the eternal death it brings—separation from God. No one, on his own, can attempt the task of teaching the Gospel, knowing the awesome consequences it brings to those who hear and reject it.

FOOD FOR THOUGHT: (f). If no one can teach the Gospel on his own, how were Paul, the Apostles, and others through the ages able to accomplish this task?

2:17. For we are not, as so many, peddling the word of God; but as of sincerity, but as from God, we speak in the sight of God in Christ. In spite of the claims of his detractors, Paul's mission is to teach the truth that Christ brought to the world, not to bring glory or material profit to himself—as is the case with many false teachers (2 Pet 2:1). The great apostolic mission of the Church is to continue this work. Accordingly, every person who considers himself a Christian is called upon to learn the fullness of Christ's teachings, to live by them and to pass them on to others. By permission of God, the Devil has power and dominion in this world, as he will until Christ returns in glory. No area of life on earth is beyond Satan's reach. Wherever God's work is being done, Satan tries especially hard to spread divisiveness (Rev 12:17).

Evil originates...in the spiritual sin of the angel. And the attitude of Lucifer reveals to us the root of every sin: pride as revolt against God. He who was first called to deification by grace wished to be God by himself. The root of sin is thus the thirst for self-deification, the hatred of grace. Remaining dependent on God in his very

> being, since his being was created by God, the spirit in revolt consequently acquires a hatred of being, a frenzy to destroy, a thirst for an impossible nothingness. As only the earthly world remains open to him, he tries here to destroy the divine plan, and having failed to annihilate creation, to disfigure it. The drama that began in Heaven continues on earth, as the faithful angels close the gates of Heaven unyieldingly to the fallen angels.[9]

It is not surprising, therefore, that throughout its history the Church has been plagued by those who have misused the Gospel for personal gain and glory on earth, rather than to bring people to Christ. Those who sincerely desire to teach God's word or to do His work, in any capacity, must be careful that they do not fall into Satan's trap in this regard. To the extent that we are rewarded by the world for this work we can expect no reward in Heaven (Mt 6:1-4). This serves to encourage spiritual growth and the realization that what matters most is not what the world thinks of us but our relationship with God, and what He knows about us.

CHAPTER TWO
Food For Thought Comments

2(a). How can one person's sinfulness bring sorrow to the whole Church?

Those who are Baptized in the name of the Holy Trinity are united as the Body of Christ. It is because of this fact that His redemptive acts made salvation possible for everyone. This also means, however, that one person's unrepentant sinfulness brings sorrow to the whole Church. Sin sets up a barrier between the sinner and God. This barrier blocks the flow of grace and causes spiritual pain, anguish, and the potential of spiritual death, just as blocking the flow of blood through the body would cause serious physical problems.

> What a responsibility the Church has, to be Christ's Body, showing Him to those who are unable or unwilling to see Him in providence, or in creation! Through the Word of God lived out in the Body of Christ they can come to the Father and themselves be made again "in the likeness of God." ATHANASIUS[10]

2(b). How might a person be lost to the Church and to God's Kingdom through *too much sorrow?*

If a person was given the impression that his sinfulness could never be forgiven he could lose hope:

> ...and either do as Judas did, or live more sinfully. For if he should shrink from enduring the anguish of lengthened censure and perhaps fall into despair, he will either come to hang himself or fall into greater crimes. One ought then to take steps beforehand, lest the sore become too hard to deal with; and lest what we have done well we lose by lack of moderation. CHRYSOSTOM[11]

2(c). What is true repentance? Must we continue in despair forever about past sins?

To sin is to fall short of the mark with regard to a Christ-like way of life. True repentance is recognition of sin, followed by sorrow that one has offended God, and an attempt to change in outlook and actions to preclude further sin.

> Let us not be easy-minded afterwards, but when we transgress, afflict our minds and not merely give vent to words. For I know many who say indeed that they regret their sins but do nothing to change. They fast and wear rough garments, but are more eager for money than hucksters; fall more to anger than do wild beasts; and take more pleasure in reproach than others do in praise. These things are not repentance, these things are the semblance and shadow only of repentance, not repentance itself. CHRYSOSTOM[12]

When appropriate, the penitent should make amends with those offended, then partake of the Sacrament of Confession to draw upon the grace of forgiveness Christ entrusted to the Apostles, thus to priests of the Church, ordained through apostolic succession (Jn 20:22-23). If absolution is given by a Priest, the penitent should feel cleansed and reconciled with God, confident of His mercy. To continue in despair over confessed sins at this point is to doubt God's love, which could lead to loss of faith and *unmeasured sorrow*.

> The Devil can cause destruction even under the show of piety. He can destroy not only by leading into sin, but even by the opposite: the unmeasured sorrow following repentance for it. Then he uses not only his weapons against us but our own too. For he is not content with striking down by sin, but even by repentance he does this, unless we are vigilant. To take by sin is his proper work; by repentance, however, is our weapon. When even through repentance he is able to cause destruction, think how disgraceful the defeat, how he will laugh at and call us weak and pitiful, if he is able to subdue us with our own weapons. CHRYSOSTOM[13]

We should remember our past transgressions to the extent that they remind us that we are vulnerable to sin and to avoid slipping into a prideful feeling of self-righteousness, but we should not let sincerely repented and confessed sins bog us down. Sin prevents us from acting in love freely, which is our God-given potential. To be loosed from the bonds of sin is to be truly joyful, free to be what God wants us to be—holy.

2(d). Think about the fact that even Paul experienced moments of despondency. What can we learn from his example (vs 2:14) in coping during difficult times in our lives?

When Paul experienced difficult times, he sought comfort, consolation and advice from those who understood his mission. Ultimately though, he relied on God in all things. When he was able to lose himself in his work, he was revitalized and found the strength and courage to continue. Each Christian can find similar comfort from the never-ending Source, for each of us, in some way, is meant to be a teacher of the Gospel to those around us, most importantly through example. No matter what our circumstances might be, as long as we have the gift of life we can show God we love Him and want to be with Him forever. We do this by trying to follow the road to Him ourselves and by trying to bring others to it. When we put everything in this perspective, we realize that every difficulty in life is temporary and every hurdle surmountable.

2(e). Have you asked yourself what type of aroma your life emits to God?

Just as we leave a distinctive scent in our wake when we wear perfume, and our personality creates a certain atmosphere around us, our spiritual life—or lack of it—creates an aroma discernible to God and to those who are spiritually attuned. Wherever we go, whatever we do, our actions and demeanor should create a *sweet aroma to the Lord*. Those who visit our homes should be able to tell by what they see, what they hear and what we do that we are Christians.

> We must therefore offer ourselves as an offering to God, and in all things be found pleasing to our Maker, with an upright heart, with sincere faith, well grounded in hope, fervent in charity, offering Him the firstfruits of His own

> creation. This Pure Oblation the Church alone offers to the Creator, offering it to Him from His own creation, with giving of thanks.
>
> IRENAEUS[14]

2(f). If no one can teach the Gospel on his/her own, how were Paul, the Apostles and others like them through the ages able to accomplish this task?

Only through the grace of God could anyone carry out the task of teaching the Gospel (see 1 Cor 15:10). Thus all who desire to teach others the transforming truths about Christ, whether a spouse or parent in the home, a fellow traveler on the road through life or a priest in the pulpit—all need to pray for divine assistance.

> Were the Apostles not men such as you? Did they not dwell among men? Did they not have the same interests as you? Did they not do the same things? Perhaps you think they were angels? That they came down from Heaven? No! "But," you will say, "they worked miracles!" It was not because of their miracles that they were remarkable. How long must we speak of miracles to cover up our own laziness? Look at the lives of the Saints. They shone forth, but not because of their miracles. For many who even cast out devils are not honored because they did evil and for this were punished. What then you may ask was it that made them great? Their rejection of wealth, contempt of vainglory, and their turning away from the things of this world. Because had they been wanting in this regard, or had they indulged their passions, then even had they raised thousands from death to life they would have been not merely worthless but would have been considered frauds. Behold then that it is their life which shines forth in every way and draws down on them the grace of the Spirit.
>
> CHRYSOSTOM[15]

An effort to bring a person to knowledge and understanding of salvation through Christ will bear most fruit if it is approached not as an intellectual exercise but as a spiritual pursuit which involves both body and soul. This requires the use of spiritual tools such as prayer, fasting and the Sacraments as well as the tools of knowledge.

Let us return to the word which has been handed down to us from the beginning, watchful in prayer (1 Pet 4:7) and persevering in fasting. POLYCARP[16]

CHAPTER THREE

The Glorious Call to Holiness

BACKGROUND: Chapter Two ended with Paul's assurances that his motives for teaching the Gospel of Jesus Christ reach beyond the earthly life, into eternity. Now he offers proof of this fact.

3:1. Do we begin again to commend ourselves? Or do we need, as some others, epistles of commendation to you or letters of commendation from you? The early Church was plagued with many adversaries. Outside were pagans (who worshipped idols) and Jews (who, for the most part, rejected Christ as the Messiah). There were also troublesome factions within the Church, which consisted of those whom Paul called *false apostles* (2 Cor 11:13-15). Some of these false apostles tried to make themselves leaders for their own personal gain; some misunderstood the Gospel and taught heresy; others were Judaizers: Jews who believed Christ to be the Messiah but still thought it necessary to conform to the legalism of the Mosaic Law. Paul expresses concern that some may think he is boasting when he compares his ministry with those factions in Corinth which adversely affect the Church. His intent is not to parade his accomplishments but to make it clear that he does not need letters of recommendation explaining who he is and what he does, as he did before his conversion when he was one of the Jews from Jerusalem with the mission of persecuting Christians (Acts 9:1-2).

3:2. You are our epistle written in our hearts, known and read by all men; The very presence of the Church in Corinth is Paul's commendation. That infamous pagan city was notorious for the love of pleasure and lack of morals among its people. Yet, after learning the Gospel from Paul, many there responded to it and underwent an amazing transformation to the Christian lifestyle. This fact is proof of the validity of Paul's work as an Apostle.

3:3. you are manifestly an epistle of Christ, ministered by us, written not with ink but by the Spirit of the living God, not on tablets of stone but on tablets of flesh, that is, of the heart.

He contrasts his message with that of the Jews—the Gospel with the "Law." The Ten Commandments, part of the Written Covenant of the Old Testament, were given by God to Moses on tablets of stone (Ex 31:18). The new, final, Blood Covenant between God and man was revealed to the Corinthians by Paul but was written in the hearts of the receptive by the Holy Spirit (Jer 31:31-33). God can use each of us as an instrument to teach the Gospel, but our work will bear fruit only with those whose hearts are open to the divine.

3:4-5. And we have such trust through Christ toward God. Not that we are sufficient of ourselves to think of anything as being from ourselves, but our sufficiency is from God... Paul puts his trust in God's final covenant with man, which operates through the saving actions of Christ. He does all he can as his part of this pact but knows that without the grace of God he can do nothing. All who try to do God's work will succeed only if they do their best with the gifts God has given them and trust Him to do the rest.

3:6. who also made us sufficient as ministers of the new covenant, not of the letter but of the spirit; for the letter kills, but the Spirit gives life. The Written Covenant contained not only the Ten Commandments but 613 laws. God's people were required to follow each law to *the letter*—an impossibility. To break one was to be guilty of breaking them all (Jas 2:10), with the result that not even great luminaries such as Moses, Solomon or John the Baptist could find salvation through this covenant. Only Enoch, who lived before the giving of the Law (Gen 5:24, Heb 11:5), and Elijah, who lived during the time it was in force (2 Kings 2:1-11), did not have to pass through death. They were taken directly into God's presence because they pleased God. They were righteous, not in the complete, death-defeating sense that Christ was, but rather, in relation to the time in which they lived.[1] Enoch and Elijah point to the certainty of eternal life for man and prefigure those who will be alive at Christ's Second Coming, so will not have to pass through death.

> But many ask where Enoch was translated, and why he was translated, and why he did not die, neither he nor

> Elijah, and if they are still alive, how they live and in what form. But to ask these things is superfluous. ...For the Scriptures say nothing more than is necessary. Enoch's translation took place immediately at the beginning, and thereby the human soul received a hope of the destruction of death, of the overthrow of the devil's tyranny, and that death will be no more.
>
> CHRYSOSTOM[2]

The Written Covenant was given to the people of the Hebrew nation to set them apart from others in the world as belonging to God and to give them an opportunity to show faith and love through obedience. Man's inability to follow it perfectly, as required, also illustrated the fact that no one can earn salvation on his own. Under the Law, everyone deserved death. Therefore, *the letter*, the "Law," *kills.*

> God sought to form a mind conscious of righteousness, so that being convinced in that time of our unworthiness of attaining life through our own works, it should now, through the kindness of God, be verified to us; and having made it clear that in ourselves we were unable to enter into the kingdom of God, we might through the power of God be made able....For what other thing was capable of covering our sins than His righteousness? By what other one was it possible that we, the wicked and ungodly, could be justified, than by the only Son of God? Oh sweet exchange! Oh unsearchable operation! Oh benefits surpassing all expectation! That the wickedness of many should be hid in a single righteous One, and that the righteousness of One should justify many transgressors.
>
> MATHETES[3]

The first chapter of the Book of Genesis reveals God's original intent for man: fellowship with Him. Adam and Eve had the opportunity to pursue this potential unhampered if they would obey the one commandment He gave them. When they succumbed to Satan's voice urging them to do things his way—instant gratification of their desires—they found themselves on a path away from God, and the agony of man began. Still, God's hope for man remained the same—but now required a Savior to rescue him from his perilous downward spiral. In God's subsequent dealings with man, some responded to Him and others rejected Him, preferring false gods. Through His Oral Covenant with Abraham and His Written Covenant with Moses and the Hebrew nation, He prepared the family of David to receive the Messiah and purified special people for important roles in His plan to put man back on the road to union with his Maker.

> The history of the Old Testament is that of elections linked to successive falls. Through these God saves a "remnant" whose patient waiting purifies: through the very dialectic of disappointments, the awaiting of the triumphal Messiah becomes that of the Suffering Servant of Yahweh, the awaiting of the political liberation of a people, that of the spiritual liberation of humanity. The more God recedes, the more man's goal is universalized: until the supreme purity of the Virgin is capable of giving birth to the Savior of humanity.[4]

The old Written Covenant prefigured and was fulfilled by the new Blood Covenant. Jesus Christ fulfilled the old through obedience and ushered in the new. Instead of returning directly to God, bypassing death as did Enoch and Elijah, He allowed Himself to be put to death, though He was sinless, thus offering Himself as the Lamb of God, the last living sacrifice under the Law, which required atonement for sin (Gen 22:8, 1 Pet 1:18-19). Christ's death was not a price God had set for man's sin, nor was it a price Satan had a right to demand. His death was, however, engineered by Satan as part of his continuing attempt to deny to as many as possible that which he and the celestial beings who followed him in rebellion had lost for themselves (Rev 12:7-9). God allowed the Devil this liberty because He knew that through it Satan would be caught in his own trap. In bringing to death one who did not deserve it, Satan overstepped his bounds—he went too far.

Death could not hold Christ because He was sinless. He thus achieved victory over death. He also became the *first fruits* of the dead (1 Cor 15:20): the first to be resurrected, never to die again. His Resurrection is assurance that there is life after death; thus it offers strength and courage to those who hope for eternal life with God for themselves and their loved ones.

> As long as sin sentenced only the guilty to death, no interference with it was possible, seeing that it had justice on its side. But when it subjected to the same punishment Him Who was innocent, guiltless and worthy of crowns of honor and hymns of praise, being convicted of injustice, it was by necessary consequence stripped of its power. CYRIL OF ALEXANDRIA[5]

Those who are a part of the mystical Body of Christ through Baptism and a life of faith also cannot be held by death when it comes to them. Because they share His victory, they only pass through death, to God's presence. And while they are alive they are not bound by *the letter* of the Law—literally having to be perfect according to its tenets. Rather, they are willingly bound by love to its *spirit*, which turns man to Christ and accomplishes what the Law could not: righteousness which springs from a heart softened by love and grace.

> The Law is the shadow of the Gospel and the Gospel is the image of the good things to come. For the former checks bad activities and the latter provides good actions.
> MAXIMUS THE CONFESSOR[6]

After Christ's Crucifixion, the terms of God's covenant with man changed radically as far as what God provides and what He requires from us. He not only sent His Son to accomplish what we cannot—objectively earn our own salvation—He also gave us a partner to help us fulfill the commitment and spiritual growth He does expect from those who desire union with Him: the indwelling Holy Spirit.

> In the Law, he that has sin is punished; under the Gospel, he that has sins comes and is Baptized and is made righteous, and being made righteous, he lives, being delivered from the death of sin. The Law, if it lay hold on a murderer, puts him to death; the Gospel, if it lay hold on a murderer, enlightens and gives him life. And why do I single out a murderer? The Law laid hold on one that gathered sticks on a Sabbath day and stoned him (Num 15:32,36). This is the meaning of *the letter kills*. The Gospel takes hold of thousands of murderers

and robbers, and Baptizing delivers them from their former vices. This is the meaning of *the Spirit gives life.*
CHRYSOSTOM[7]

FOOD FOR THOUGHT: (a). What are some of the other ways in which the precepts of the Old Testament prefigured and were fulfilled by those of the New Testament? (b). Under the secular law of our land, murderers are sometimes put to death, as they were under the Mosaic Law of the Old Testament. How does this fact correlate with the Gospel, which Chrysostom writes "enlightens the murderer and gives him life"? (c). Which Orthodox icon illustrates the fact that before Christ died to redeem man from his sins there was no access to the Kingdom of Heaven? (d). How does knowledge of the Written Covenant of the Old Testament help us in our walk with Christ?

3:7-8. But if the ministry of death, written and engraved on stones, was glorious, so that the children of Israel could not look steadily at the face of Moses because of the glory of his countenance, which glory was passing away, how will the ministry of the Spirit not be more glorious? The Ten Commandments condemned man to death and separation from God because of man's sinfulness and his inability to follow them perfectly as required. The Written Covenant brought death, not because it caused sin but because it defined sin. Yet this old covenant was glorious because it was a part of God's overall divine plan for the salvation of mankind, which He revealed to His people in stages. Therefore, when Moses came down from the mountain after having received the Commandments from God engraved on tablets of stone, *the skin of his face shone*. Aaron and the people were *afraid to come near him* (Ex 34:30) because he radiated divine glory. However, the glory that shone in Moses' face would fade when he was away from God's presence, symbolizing the fact that this covenant was not permanent. Paul's point here is that if a transient covenant was so glorious that its radiance shone on Moses' face, imagine the degree of glory that is attendant to the permanent Blood Covenant through Jesus Christ, which is written in man's hearts *by the Spirit of the living God* (2 Cor 3:3).

> The children of Israel could not look directly at Moses' face, a mark of their great weakness and grovelling spirit...seeing that even of a glory that is to be done away, or rather is in comparison no glory at all, they were not able to be spectators. CHRYSOSTOM[8]

3:9. For if the ministry of condemnation had glory, the ministry of righteousness exceeds much more in glory. As part of the family of fallen man, we were born with a tendency toward sin. Through faith that Christ is the Messiah, our Savior according to God's divine plan, we rise above this sinful nature and are saved from the condemnation of being found guilty by the Law. As part of the Body of Christ through Baptism, we take on Christ's righteousness before God—partake of divine nature (2 Pet 1:4)—if, as we are able, we try to live Christ-like lives: our profession of faith. Faith, expressing itself in the attempt to be obedient, is the activator. He who demonstrates faith is aided by the Holy Spirit towards growth in holiness in the image of Christ. This is the *ministry of righteousness*, which is more glorious than the *ministry of condemnation* of the Old Testament because it leads to eternal life.

> Since then the Spirit has given us life, let us remain living and not return again to the former deadness: for *Christ dies no more; for the death that He died, He died unto sin once* (Rom 6:9-10) and He will not have us always saved by grace: for so we would be empty of all things. Therefore, He asks us to contribute something also from ourselves. Let us then contribute and preserve to the soul its life. CHRYSOSTOM[9]

If our lives demonstrate faith as our part of the Blood Covenant with God, we walk toward eternal life with Him. The inevitable sins committed along the way (succumbed to unwittingly through weakness of flesh or immaturity of faith rather than indifference to or rejection of God) are forgiven through repentance/Confession. On the other hand, if our lives do not show faith, we walk in a direction that takes us away from God eternally. Only these two options are open. There will be no respite from the agony endured by those who cut themselves off from God through lack of faith because *Christ dies no more*: there will be no additional atoning sacrifice for those who do not recognize and respond to "the single, all encompassing and unrepeatable one that Christ offered once (Heb 9:28)."[10]

> Groan when you have sinned, not because you are to be punished (for this is nothing), but because you have offended your Master, one so gentle, one so kind, one Who loves you so and longs for your salvation so that He gave even His Son for you. For this groan, and do this continually: for this is Confession. CHRYSOSTOM[11]

Each of us has one opportunity—our lifetime—to show faith in God's divine plan for the salvation of mankind through Jesus Christ. The required life of attempted obedience is not easy but not impossible either because of the grace to which God has given man access.

> Our body, before Christ's coming, was an easy prey to the assaults of sin. For after man's fall a great swarm of passions entered also. And for this cause it was not nimble for running the race of virtue. For there was no Spirit present to assist, nor any baptism of power to mortify (Jn 7:39). But as some horse that answered not the rein, it ran indeed, but made frequent slips, the Law meanwhile announcing what was to be done and what not, yet not conveying to those in the race anything over and above exhortation by means of words. But when Christ had come, the effort became easier and, therefore, we had a more distant goal set us, in that the assistance given us was greater...Unless we stoop down very low to it, sin will not get the better of us...for grace remitted our former sins and secures us against future ones.
>
> CHRYSOSTOM[12]

FOOD FOR THOUGHT: (e). A person may have life in his body yet be dead spiritually. What are the signs of death of the soul? ...of life in the soul?

3:10-11. For even what was made glorious had no glory in this respect, because of the glory that excels. For if what is passing away was glorious, what remains is much more glorious. Though the old covenant had glory, by comparison with the new it had no glory at all—as the brightness of the moon is dulled by the rising of the sun.

3:12-13. Therefore, since we have such hope, we use great boldness of speech—unlike Moses, who put a veil over his face so that the children of Israel could not look steadily at the end of what was passing away. Because the glory that shone in Moses' face would fade with time after he left the presence of God, he put a veil over his face after he spoke to the people of Israel so they would not notice and become disheartened. Paul has nothing to hide. The glory of the final Blood Covenant is not temporary—nothing will replace it. On the contrary, it is a glory which will increase, reaching its fulfillment at the Second Coming of Christ. Therefore, he is bold in proclaiming it.

> **FOOD FOR THOUGHT:** (f). Why did Moses' face shine (Ex 34:30), rather than the tablets upon which God had written the Ten Commandments?

3:14-15. But their minds were hardened. For until this day the same veil remains unlifted in the reading of the Old Testament, because the veil is taken away in Christ. But even to this day, when Moses is read, a veil lies on their heart. The Hebrew nation in general did not recognize Christ as the Messiah when He announced the new covenant—the fulfillment of the old. It knew the letter of the Law but did not understand its life giving spirit: that the Savior would come to release them from its bondage. It looked instead, as it still does, for a messiah to lead them to perfect conditions on earth rather than in Heaven with God. *Their minds were hardened*, that is, they were not *meek* (Mt 5:5), the Hebrew word for which means, "capable of being molded." To be one of God's people we must be willing to let God mold us according to His image—and try with all our might to live according to His truths. A synergistic effort between God and man is required. The minds of the unenlightened Hebrew people were hardened with self-will and the truth could not penetrate. Therefore, to this day they continue to read only the Old Testament and to misunderstand it, with the result that there is still a veil between them and the truth.

> He said not, "the veil remains on the writing," but in the reading. CHRYSOSTOM[13]

That is, the fault lies not in what was written but in the way it is perceived. This is an example of the fact that Scripture can be misunderstood, which is why we must look to the Church and the truths it has preserved through the Ecumenical Councils and the consensus of the writings of the Fathers. If we give our own interpretation to Scripture, we distort it according to our own will and deprive ourselves of that which God intends to convey.

> *...their minds were hardened.* What has this to do with the veil? It prefigured what would be. For not only did they not then perceive; but they do not even now see the Law. And the fault lies with themselves, for the hardness is that of an unimpressible and perverse judgment...For if the Law was brought to an end by Christ, which it was, and the Law said this by anticipation, how will they who do not receive Christ, Who has done away with the Law, see that the Law was done away? Being incapable of seeing this, it is very plain that even of the Law itself which asserted these things, they do not know the power nor the full glory[14]...for the glory of the Law is to turn men to Christ. CHRYSOSTOM[15]

Those who recognized and accepted Jesus Christ as the Son of God and their Messiah removed the veil from their hearts and their minds.

> **FOOD FOR THOUGHT:** (g). What Biblical event symbolized this removal of the veil between God's people and the truth?

It is important to remember, however, that our roots as God's people are in Judaism; that Jesus, the Apostles and all the first Christians were Jews; and that those of Hebrew heritage who accept Christ as their Messiah are still His "chosen people," *natural branches* called first to introduce God's truths to the world (read Romans 11). It is good, therefore, to try to share the Gospel with them and with all people of the world whenever possible, as Paul did. When he entered a town he would first go to the local synagogue to tell the Jews that the Messiah they had been waiting for had arrived. Then he would go wherever Gentiles gathered, to preach the Gospel (Acts 18:4-6).

3:16. Nevertheless when one turns to the Lord, the veil is taken away. Exodus 34:34-35 relates that when Moses returned to the presence of the Lord he removed the veil from his face, an act symbolic of the fact that when one actively turns to God, he receives understanding. Chrysostom says this verse also points to the general conversion of the nation of Israel,[16] which is one of the signs of the imminence of the Second Coming of Christ (see Rom 11:19-32 & Is 59:20).

> *When the fullness of the Gentiles has come in...all Israel will be saved* (Rom 11:26), at the time of His Second Coming and the end of the world. CHRYSOSTOM[17]

When the Jews, as a people, hardened their hearts with regard to Christ, His Gospel was brought to those not bound by the Law. At a time known only by God, when the number of Gentiles to be saved has been reached, He will soften the hearts of the people of Israel and they will *turn to the Lord.* They will begin to comprehend the message of the Old Testament: that Jesus Christ is the promised Messiah Who came to rescue them from the futility of looking to the Law for salvation. They will remove the veil from their faces. They will turn from the letter to the Spirit and will understand.

3:17. Now the Lord is the Spirit; and where the Spirit of the Lord is, there is liberty. The Lord to Whom the children of Israel must turn is the same Lord into Whose presence Moses went to receive the Ten Commandments. But He wants them now to have a fuller understanding of Him, as a triune God. Through them God revealed the truth that there is only one God—one Creator—not many gods as the pagans thought. He gave them indications of His tripartite fullness through the Old Testament (i.e., Gen 1:26: *Then God said, "Let **us** make man in **our** image, according to **our** likeness;"* Gen 18:1-3: *Abraham looked up and saw **three** men. He ran from the tent door to meet **them** and bowed himself to the earth and said, **"My Lord..."***). In time, the Incarnation and

Transfiguration revealed the person of God the Son; Who revealed the person of God the Holy Spirit (Jn 15:26); Who, in turn, breathed life into the Church at Pentecost (Acts 2). Since then, when the Holy Spirit leads a person to Christ, he is led to God the Father (Jn 14:6) and through this Holy Trinity receives liberty from the bondage and condemnation of the Law. He finds himself free, as Adam had been, to grow in communion with God.

3:18. But we all, with unveiled face, beholding as in a mirror the glory of the Lord, are being transformed into the same image from glory to glory, just as by the Spirit of the Lord. Love makes man a willing slave (Rom 6:22). With liberty from the Law and a fuller understanding of God, those who have committed their lives to Christ are able to look upon His glory and to become reflectors of that glory to the extent of their faith and love.

> As soon as we are baptized the soul beams even more than the sun, being cleansed by the Spirit; and not only do we behold the glory of God but from it also receive a sort of splendor. Just as if pure silver is turned toward the sun's rays, it will itself also shoot forth rays, not from its own natural property only but also from the solar lustre; so also does the soul, being cleansed and made brighter than silver, receive a ray from the glory of the Spirit and send it back. CHRYSOSTOM[18]

In this present life, with the veil removed for true Christians, we can see God and His divine plan for our salvation, though still only indirectly. We see them as through a mirror, which only reflects reality. Because of the dazzling brilliance of the sun, the human eye cannot look directly at it without damage. When a solar eclipse occurs, the moon is positioned between the sun and the earth. During this phenomenon, much or most of the sun's brilliant light is blocked by the moon, but still the sun's rays are so powerful that we are cautioned not to look at it directly but through a device which allows a view but deflects its power. In similar fashion, God and His divine plan are so glorious that we are unable to have first-hand knowledge of them but are given reflected glimpses in proportion to our zeal and spiritual maturity. As we strive to be obedient—demonstrating faith—we are transformed and continually grow in His image *from glory to glory*, that is, from one glorious state of spiritual growth in holiness and awareness of God to another, through the help of the Holy Spirit.

> When the mind of man...is raised on high and sees the Word, and in Him also the Father of the Word, it takes pleasure in contemplating Him and gains renewal by its desire toward Him...as Adam is described in the Holy Scriptures as having at the beginning had his mind Godward in a freedom unembarrassed by shame and as associating with the holy ones in that contemplation of things perceived by the mind which he enjoyed in the place where he was—the place the holy Moses called in figure a Garden. So purity of soul is sufficient of itself to reflect God, as the Lord also says, *Blessed are the pure in heart, for they shall see God.* ATHANASIUS[19]

FOOD FOR THOUGHT: (h). Why are the stages of spiritual growth called *glorious*?

CHAPTER THREE

Food For Thought Comments

3(a). What are some of the ways in which the precepts of the Old Testament prefigured and were fulfilled by those of the New Testament?

(1). Old Testament sacrifices were commanded by God from those guilty of breaking the Law to teach man that sin required atonement (see Books of Exodus, Leviticus, Numbers and Deuteronomy). They pointed to and were fulfilled by the sacrifice of Jesus Christ, the Lamb of God, the last living sacrifice, Who gave His life to redeem mankind from his sins once and for all.

(2). The Hebrew Passover (Ex 12:1-14) was instituted by God when He sent the angel of death, who "passed over" (and thus did not bring death to) the first-born of the homes marked by the blood of the lamb according to divine instruction. This first Passover prefigured the New Passover (1 Cor 5:7): the shedding of the Blood of the Lamb of God, Jesus Christ. Those marked as God's people by the Blood of Christ (through Eucharist) will not be held by death. They pass through death to eternal life with God.

(3). That which was called the "Feast of Weeks" in the Old Testament (Lev 23:15-22) was the Hebrew Pentecost. It commemorated God's giving of the Ten Commandments to Moses and the harvest from the new land. Hebrew Pentecost prefigured Christian Pentecost (the descent of the Holy Spirit and the resultant harvest of souls brought to faith). Christian Pentecost occurred fifty days after Christ's Resurrection, on the very day the Jews were observing their Pentecost (Acts 2:1-4).

(4). The Old Testament commanded that the Sabbath (Saturday), the day upon which God rested from His work of creation, be kept holy (Gen 2:2-3, Ex 20:8-11). The Old Testament Sabbath prefigured the Great and Holy Sabbath when Christ rested in the Tomb following His Crucifixion. In turn, Christ's Resurrection on Sunday, the Lord's Day (Rev 1:10), prefigures life in the Kingdom for those in-Christ. The Sabbath continues to be honored as a day of preparation for the Lord's Day (Gr: Kyriaki): the day on which Christians worship God and profess faith in Christ's Resurrection and hope for their own.

(5). Under the Oral Covenant with Abraham, circumcision was required as a sign of belonging to the One, True God (Gen 17:10-12). It was required on the *eighth* day of life—the day with properties beyond this world for God's people. Circumcision pointed to and was superseded by Baptism as the sign of belonging to Christ: in submitting oneself or one's child to this Mystery obediently, faith is demonstrated (see Mt 28:18-19, Acts 2:38-39, 15:1-29).

> It is possible for us to show how the eighth day [Sunday/ the Lord's Day] possessed a certain mysterious import, which the seventh day did not possess and which was promulgated by God through these rites...
>
> The blood of that circumcision is obsolete, and we trust in the blood of salvation; there is now another covenant, and another law has gone forth from Zion. Jesus Christ circumcises all who will...with knives of stone[20];that they may be a righteous nation, a people keeping faith, holding to the truth, and maintaining peace.
>
> JUSTIN THE MARTYR[21]

(6). The priesthood of the Old Testament, established through Moses' brother Aaron, of the tribe of Levi, offered sacrifices in the Temple on behalf of the people to atone for sin (Ex 28-29). This Levitical priesthood pointed to and was superseded by the high priesthood of Christ Himself after the order of Melchizedek (Gen 14:18, Ps 110:4, Heb 7), which is eternal. This is the priesthood in which males in the Orthodox Church who receive a calling from God participate (Mk 3:14-15, Mt 28:16-20, Acts 6:2-6). The Church, comprised of the faithful, is the Body of Christ; the priest is the image of Christ, the Head of the Body. As such, the priest continually offers to God, sacramentally, the one, final blood sacrifice of Christ in redemption of the sins of mankind. The priest "can fulfill this service only because the priesthood...is not 'his'...but the one and same indivisible priesthood of Christ, which eternally lives and is eternally fulfilled in the Church, the Body of Christ."[22]

3(b). Under the Law of the Old Testament, murderers were put to death, as they sometimes are under the secular law of our land. How does this fact correlate with the Gospel, which Chrysostom writes "enlightens the murderer and gives him life"?

There is no easy answer to the question of capital punishment. The early Church condemned it but soon realized that, like war, it was sometimes necessary—to protect the innocent and the sanctity of life in general.

Life was created by God and belongs to God. Life is each person's opportunity to discover Jesus Christ, demonstrate faith in and love for Him (the criteria for salvation) and to grow in His image toward union with God. To take a life could be to short-circuit that process. The Christian ideal is to reform a criminal through love, but there are those who reject any such attempt. Some may be brought to a state of repentance only by the realization that they face death. This prospect, which offers time to prepare, affords a criminal the opportunity to make peace with God (a chance denied murder victims). Also, the sincerity of contrition and change is difficult for any human being or council to judge.

The sixth commandment prohibits murder (Ex 20:13), but Mosaic Law did not strike out the death penalty (Ex 21:12-17). Capital punishment is not murder but authorized killing, which the State has the right to enforce (Rom 13:4). To maintain a civilized society, those guilty of disobeying the secular laws of the land must face the consequences. Christ taught that secular authority is given by God and should be obeyed (Mt 22:21, Jn 19:11). Coming to terms with capital punishment could encourage society to reflect on the fact that actions bring consequences—in this life and the next.

There should, however, be no rush to kill. Christian principles call for a system of law which, first and foremost, emphasizes reform and rehabilitation of the criminal. The law which deems this unattainable or inappropriate because of the heinousness of a particular crime must guard against mistakes and be fair to all. Capital punishment should not be a part of the penal code unless it is used equitably across the board, not just against those whom society does not value and those who cannot afford an expensive defense .[23]

No one, however, is ever excluded from the power of the Gospel. Till the moment of death, anyone can call upon the mercy of God. Like the thief on the cross (Lk 23:39-43), he who acknowledges his sin and repents, though he lose his earthly life, may, subject to Christ's judgment of the sincerity of his faith, receive forgiveness and eternal life with God.

3(c). Which Orthodox icon illustrates the fact that there was no access to the Kingdom of Heaven before Christ died to redeem man from sin?

The Icon of Christ's Descent into Hades, also known as the Icon of the Resurrection (see page 66), depicts the truth that before Christ's Crucifixion, no one (except Enoch and Elijah) entered Heaven (read Heb 11, especially verses 13,39-40). It portrays the fact that while Christ's Body lay in the Tomb, His Soul descended into Hades[24] (1 Pet 3:18-20; 4:6; Eph 4:9-10) to gather all who, before He came to earth, tried to live righteously while waiting for the Messiah to rescue them from the despair of being unable to earn salvation for themselves by following the Law to the letter. At His descent, they (and in the case of non-Jews, those who tried to live according to what they had been able to discover about God) were given the opportunity to accept Him as Lord. This was not a second chance but the opportunity they had not had during their lifetime. Symbolizing these truths, the icon depicts Adam and Eve being taken from the throes of death. Also depicted as having been liberated are Kings David and Solomon, Abraham, John the Baptist, Abel, and the Prophets: Old and New Testament figures who point to Him in the icon as the Messiah they waited during their lives. The figure shown in the blackness at the bottom of this icon symbolizes the Devil.[25] Through His Crucifixion, Christ put Satan (and death) in chains, restrained them (Rev 20:2). That is, the power the Devil had over mankind after man's sin was death, but the sting of death was now dispelled, for though man would still have to pass through death (until the Second Coming), Christ's Resurrection proved death would not be final to those who died truly believing in Him.

Christ's Descent Into Hades

> The Fathers, however justly they lived until the Coming of the Lord, were not brought into the Kingdom until He had descended Who would open the gates of Paradise by the intervention of His death; they murmured because they had lived justly in order that they might enter the Kingdom, and yet they suffered long delay. It was, therefore, they who had labored in the Vineyard, and it was they who murmured, whom the *abodes of Hell*, however peaceful, had received after their just lives. It was, therefore, after their murmuring, that they received the reward; they who after the long ages of Hell reached at length the joys of the Kingdom. We, however, who have come at the eleventh hour murmur not after our labor but receive our reward because coming into this world after the Coming of the Mediator, we are brought into the Kingdom almost as soon as we depart from our body; and we receive without any delay that which the ancient Fathers merited to receive after prolonged delay.
>
> GREGORY THE GREAT[26]

The "abodes of Hell" entered by those who had tried to live righteously according to the Law while awaiting the Messiah are said to have been "peaceful" because they were the regions of Hell furthest from the realm of Satan. Just as those who belong to God differ in their proximity to Him in the Kingdom according to their relationship with Him, those in Hell are estranged from God on the same basis.

3(d). How does knowledge of the Written Covenant of the Old Testament help us in our walk with Christ?

Having knowledge of the Written Covenant of the Old Testament aids our understanding of the fullness of God's divine plan for mankind and the reason we needed a Savior. As our awareness of the magnitude of what Christ did for us grows, so will our love for and obedience to Him.

3(e). A person may have life in his body, yet be dead spiritually. What are the signs of death of the soul? ...life in the soul?

Signs of death of the soul are such as we see in the rich man of the parable (Lk 16:19-31):

> ...who ate and drank and lived in pleasure only....When the soul does not perform the things proper to it, is it not dead? When, for instance, it has no care for virtue, but is rapacious and transgresses the law. How can I tell that you have a soul? Because you walk? So do the irrational creatures. Because you eat and drink? So do the wild beasts. Because you stand upright on two feet? This tells me only that you are a beast in human form...How can I see that you have the soul of a man, when you kick like an ass, when you bear malice like the camel, when you bite like the bear, when you are ravenous like the wolf, when you steal like the fox, when you are wily as the serpent, and when you are shameless as a dog.
>
> CHRYSOSTOM[27]

Signs of life in the soul are such as we see in Lazarus, the poor man of the same parable:

> ...though wrestling with continual hunger, and not even supplied with the food that was necessary, did not speak blasphemy against God, but endured all nobly.
>
> CHRYSOSTOM[28]

3(f). Why did Moses' face shine (Ex 34:30), rather than the tablets upon which God had written the Ten Commandments?

The fact that Moses' face shone when he came down from Mount Sinai, rather than the tablets upon which God had written, points to the fact that God glorifies spiritually, in this life and in the next, those who bring glory to Him. God's light radiates through those who do His work. It is interesting to note that at first Moses was not aware that his face radiated glory—he became aware of it through the reactions of others.

> Through the glory of the Spirit that shone from his face in such a way that no one could look at it, Moses showed how in the resurrection of the righteous their bodies will be glorified with the glory that their souls already possess inwardly during this present life.
>
> MAKARIOS OF EGYPT[29]

We see this also in such phenomena as "weeping" icons, which some have been privileged to behold. In a weeping icon of the Theotokos, for instance, the focus is on her—not on the wood, paint and canvas of these icons, which are but vehicles of revelation. Through her tears, the Theotokos is recognized as having spiritual vitality because of the life of faith she lived while on earth.

3(g). What Biblical event symbolized the removal of the veil between God's people and the truth?

The tearing of the veil in the Temple in Jerusalem upon the death of Christ (Mt 27:51).

In Solomon's Temple, the Holy Place, in which a lamp of oil burned continuously (Ex 27:20-21) and incense was offered to God daily (Ex 30:6-7), was separated from the Most Holy Place by a veil (Ex 26:33, 2 Chr 3). God was present among His people in the Most Holy Place, *above the mercy seat...between the two cherubim...on the ark* which housed the Ten Commandments (Ex 25:17-22). No one could enter the Most Holy Place except the High Priest. Just once a year, on the Day of Atonement, he entered the Holy of Holies to offer sacrifice to God for the sins of the people (Heb 9:6-7). The veil symbolized the fact that because of sin man was separated from God, just as cherubim and a flaming sword were placed *at the east end of the Garden of Eden, to guard the way to the tree of life* (Gen 3:24). Through Jesus' death, which atoned once and for all for the sins of mankind, this barrier was removed, thus the veil was *torn in two*. Man once again had access to God and to everlasting life—through His Son.

3(h). Why are the stages of spiritual growth called *glorious*?

The stages of spiritual growth gradually bring us closer to our Lord in this life and to eternal life in His glorious Kingdom.

> Paul's garments wrought miracles (Acts 19:11-12); Peter's very shadows were mighty (Acts 5:15)...and those looking steadfastly at Stephen, *saw his face as the face of an angel* (Acts 6:15). But this was nothing compared to the glory flashing within. For what Moses had upon his face, these carried about with them on their souls even far

more. For the glory shining on Moses' face was more obvious to the senses, but this was incorporeal. And as shooting stars reflect their brilliance upon that which is near them, so does it also happen with the faithful. Therefore, surely they with whom it is thus are set free from earth and have their dreams of the things of Heaven. CHRYSOSTOM[30]

CHAPTER FOUR
A Purifying, Deifying Process

BACKGROUND: In Chapter Three, Paul expounded upon the glory of the new Blood Covenant between God and His people. He now writes that it is the light of this glory which sustains and energizes him during the dark moments of his ministry.

4:1. Therefore, since we have this ministry, as we have received mercy, we do not lose heart. The fact that God mercifully redirected Paul when he was following the wrong path is always in his thoughts. The wonder of it sustains him in his difficult ministry.

4:2. But we have renounced the hidden things of shame, not walking in craftiness nor handling the word of God deceitfully, but by manifestation of the truth commending ourselves to every man's conscience in the sight of God. Contrary to the accusations of his detractors, Paul does not twist the Gospel to achieve his own ends. He strives to be a living example of the type of life it commands, publicly and privately, no matter what the consequences might be.

It would seem that anyone who were to ponder the wonders of life with an open mind would eventually concede that all signs point to the existence of a divine Being—the Creator of all—Who would naturally have a comprehensive plan for man, His most magnificent creation. The next logical step for the sincere seeker of truth would be to search out and try to understand all aspects of that plan and to make the decisions of life accordingly, so as to be sure to include himself under its umbrella. When we contemplate God and His word, we cannot keep what we like and toss out what we do not, nor can we slant interpretations according to our own desires. To do so would indicate that we believe we can create our own truth and reveal a lack of real faith in the existence of God. This is the delusion of those who proclaim love for God yet insist they have the right to live in any manner they choose—while still fully expecting to go automatically to a mythical paradise of their dreams when they die.

> A young Abbot was counselled thus, in our own day, by a Holy man: "Today many people, wishing for an excuse not to do what God asks of them, find fault with the teaching of the Holy Church and reject correct Christian belief. Instead, they choose to believe what they wish. This is akin to a man not wishing to believe that he will die, simply because the notion does not comfort him. Not only will he fail to prepare for death, as one ought to do, but he will inevitably find himself in the snare of death. Correct belief is not based on what we wish were true but on Truth itself."[1]

4:3-4. But even if our Gospel is veiled, it is veiled to those who are perishing, whose minds the god of this age has blinded, who do not believe, lest the light of the Gospel of the glory of Christ, Who is the image of God, should shine on them. Paul has no secret agenda. He teaches the truth for all to hear. Some understand and accept it. Others reject it because the *god of this age*, Satan, has blinded them to the truth. They have allowed themselves to be fooled by him and grasp at any excuse to believe there is no God rather than give up the worldly distractions that cloud their vision. Each moment lived in rejection of or indifference to Christ is one moment closer to an eternal existence devoid of God's blessings.

> **FOOD FOR THOUGHT:** (a). Why is Satan called the "god" of this age (Jn 12:31, Eph 2:2)? (b). What are the enticements of the world that can lead us away from God? (c). What assistance does the Church offer to help us stay on the road to the Kingdom?

4:5. For we do not preach ourselves, but Christ Jesus the Lord, and ourselves your servants for Jesus' sake. Paul does not teach his own philosophy, nor does he slant God's word toward that which would be convenient or comfortable for him. As expected of an Apostle, he has become a servant to those he teaches in order to pass on the truths entrusted to him (Mt 20:26). A servant caters to the needs of those he serves. That which each person needs most, whether he realizes it or not, is salvation. Every Christian is obliged to try to bring the Gospel of Jesus

Christ to the unenlightened around him. We serve best if we try to determine each person's level of understanding of God and work individually from that point.

4:6-7. For it is the God Who commanded light to shine out of darkness Who has shone in our hearts to give the light of the knowledge of the glory of God in the face of Jesus Christ. But we have this treasure in earthen vessels, that the excellence of the power may be of God and not of us. The Creator of all, Who caused light to be from nothing (Gen 1), commissioned Paul to bring knowledge of Him, through the life of His Son, to those who have receptive hearts.

> Most people are like men walking at night wholly without light and not enjoying the slightest illumination in their souls from the divine Logos, so that they scarcely differ from the blind. They are totally caught up in material entanglements and the chains of temporal life, neither restrained by divine awe nor performing any virtuous acts. On the other hand, those who live in the world and are illumined by the holy commandments as by the stars, and who do cleave to God with faith and awe, are not utterly shrouded in darkness and for this reason can hope to attain salvation. MAKARIOS OF EGYPT[2]

The first man was created from the dust of the earth (Gen 2:7). Thus Paul refers to those who teach the Gospel as earthen vessels. The vessel is ordinary and weak because it easily breaks down from injury, illness, pain, fear and sin; but that which it carries is mighty, everlasting and priceless. This paradox illustrates the fact that the power of the Gospel comes not from that which carries it but from God. An understanding of this truth eliminates pride in those who do God's work.

Those who teach the Gospel of Christ do so by choice and must work very hard to achieve results, but without God's help their efforts would be in vain. God has deigned to work in partnership with man (1 Cor 3:9). Man is the tool—God provides the power.

4:8-10. We are hard pressed on every side, yet not crushed; we are perplexed, but not in despair; persecuted, but not

forsaken; struck down, but not destroyed—always carrying about in the body the dying of the Lord Jesus, that the life of Jesus also may be manifested in our body. These are words to write in our hearts. At Paul's conversion the Lord had said, *I will show him how many things he must suffer for My Name's sake* (Acts 9:16). Now Paul reflects that even though every aspect of his life and ministry have been fraught with great difficulty, he is able to continue by remembering always that Christ lived and died to give man a way back to God. Those who really understand this truth carry on His work, in spite of the tribulation it may bring.

> The one who loves Christ thoroughly imitates him as much as he can. Christ did not cease to do good to men. Treated ungratefully and blasphemed, he was patient; beaten and put to death by them, He endured, not thinking ill of anyone at all. These three are the works of love of neighbor, in the absence of which a person who says he loves Christ or possesses His Kingdom deceives himself. For He says, *Not the one who says to me "Lord, Lord," will enter the Kingdom of Heaven, but the one who does the will of my Father.*
>
> MAXIMUS THE CONFESSOR[3]

Paul persevered by remaining focused on the goal (Phil 3:14). When the travails and uncertainties of life threaten to make us veer off course, this is the only solution. With our spiritual eyes set on the glory of the Kingdom to come and with the grace of God strengthening us, we carry on. This focus may not solve all our problems, but it will prevent them from defeating us.

> When, by counsel of the serpent, Adam and Eve departed from the contemplation of God...and from desire of Him, they grew in diverse lusts and in those of the bodily senses. Next, as is apt to happen, having formed these desires, they became habituated to them, so that they were afraid to leave them. Then the soul became subject to cowardice and fear and pleasures and thoughts of mortality. For not being willing to leave her lusts, she fears death and separation from the body.
>
> ATHANASIUS[4]

4:11-12. For we who live are always delivered to death for Jesus' sake, that the life of Jesus also may be manifested in our mortal flesh. So then death is working in us, but life in you. The daily struggles Paul experienced in disciplining his will to conform to God's will allowed the divine presence and power to be demonstrated as it could in no other way. He willingly died to the ways of this world so his spiritual life through Christ would be visible to those who understood. As the book of Acts records, there had been continual plots to kill him. He had been beaten, stoned, put in stocks and driven out of cities. No one would willingly suffer as he had without having beheld the wonder of God. Again and again God allowed Paul to be thrust into circumstances in which he was beyond human help. At the same time, He showered him with grace to endure and overcome so those looking on would believe. Paul's willingness to put his fate in God's hands, even if it should lead to death, was a powerful witness which brought many to salvation through the Gospel.

4:13-14. But since we have the same spirit of faith, according to what is written, "I believed and therefore I spoke," we also believe and therefore speak, knowing that He Who raised up the Lord Jesus will also raise us up with Jesus, and will present us with you. Quoting the Psalmist (Ps 116:10), Paul expresses his compulsion to teach the Gospel in spite of danger. The truth and power of the saving message of Jesus Christ cannot be restrained. To believe requires action based on that belief. It is incongruous, impossible, to really believe that through Christ we have eternal salvation and not to speak out about it and have that fact affect our life, our decisions.

> Would you think it right if the perishable glory of worldly things were gained only after great toil and sweat by those who seek them, while to reign endlessly with Christ and to enjoy inexpressible blessings was something to be gained cheaply and easily, and could be attained without labor and effort by anyone who wished?
>
> MAKARIOS OF EGYPT[5]

Paul knows that death can come at any time. He does not seek it but does not let fear of it guide his actions. He carries on, doing whatever is necessary to propagate the Gospel. If death should come in the course of this life of obedience, he will face it willingly. His complete faith in the Resurrection of Christ assures him that there will be a universal Resurrection, after which all true Christians will be together *with Jesus*. This was the overriding thought always present in the minds of the early Christians.

> Do you not see them exposed to wild beasts, that they may be persuaded to deny the Lord, and yet not overcome? Do you not see that the more of them are punished, the greater becomes the number of the rest? This does not seem to be the work of man: this is the power of God; these are the evidences of His manifestation.
>
> MATHETES[6]

If we keep this same thought in our hearts and minds always, it will comfort and strengthen us and urge us to continue the life in Christ, however different that may make us from those around us. Guided by this truth, nothing can separate us from the love of God (Rom 8:37-39).

> Grant us, O Lord, to imitate the watchfulness of those who waited for Your Resurrection, so that day and night our souls may be turned towards you.
>
> EPHRAEM THE SYRIAN[7]

4:15. For all things are for your sakes, that grace, having spread through the many, may cause thanksgiving to abound to the glory of God. Everything Paul does to teach the Gospel has as its goal the hope that as many as possible will come to know and to love Christ. Those who are thus awakened attract divine grace from God to direct them in Christ-like lives. Transformed by this process, they are exceedingly grateful to have been directed toward this glorious pursuit—the purpose for life—and give rightful glory to God for His great mercy.

4:16. Therefore we do not lose heart. Even though our outward man is perishing, yet the inward man is being renewed day by day. Suffering for the sake of the Gospel is taking its toll on Paul's body, the *outward man*, but he presses on because this same suffering is causing his soul, the *inward man*, to be purified, strengthened and molded in the image of Christ. The inward man —that which endures forever—is thus renewed.

> ...by faith, by hope, by a forward will; finally, by braving hardships. For in proportion to the sufferings of the body, the soul has higher hopes and becomes brighter, like gold refined in the fire more and more.
>
> CHRYSOSTOM[8]

This verse can also be applied to the earthly process of aging. Growing old, for many, is very difficult. To see their hair turn white, wrinkles appear and vigor diminish is traumatic because these things are reminders of the inevitability of death. A true Christian, however, knows that for the one who loves God, the most important aspect of life on earth is that it offers the way to the eternal Kingdom. Therefore, when the outward man shows signs of aging, he who is confident of spiritual growth of the inward man in the image of Christ does not despair; he takes comfort and joy in knowing that he walks not toward death but beyond death toward God. S/he actually improves with age: the inner person grows in holiness as the outer person declines.

> Such is the beauty of the soul; even in old age it has many enamored of it, and it never fades but blooms forever. In order then that we also may gain this beauty, let us go in quest of those that have it and be enamored of them. For so shall we too be able, when we have attained this beauty, to obtain the good things eternal.
>
> CHRYSOSTOM[9]

FOOD FOR THOUGHT: (d). What qualities in those involved in the difficulties of life cause renewed faith in those around them? What qualities create doubt and fear in others?

4:17. For our light affliction, which is but for a moment, is working for us a far more exceeding and eternal weight of glory... Life on earth, however long it may be, is very short—but a moment—as compared to eternity. The difficulties we encounter while trying to live according to our faith in Christ are necessary to prove that we do indeed believe in Him and to mold us in His image. They are *light*, easy to bear, when compared to the glory of being with God eternally (Romans 8:18).

> In this life there is an equal portion of toils and reward; and often, on the contrary, the toil is endless while the fruit is little, or not even a little; but in the case of the Kingdom, the labor is little while the pleasure is great and boundless. CHRYSOSTOM[10]

4:18. while we do not look at the things which are seen, but at the things which are not seen. For the things which are seen are temporary, but the things which are not seen are eternal. The visible elements of this world, as beautiful as they may be or as ugly as they have become, are temporary. Their overriding value is what they tell us of what is unseen. The sun rising and setting without fail to sustain life on earth reminds us that we have a Heavenly Father Who created everything visible and invisible and Who cares about His creation, providing man with everything he needs to fulfill the purpose for life. The continual corruption of that which was created "good" (Gen 1:31) reminds us that we have choices to make in this life. These choices have consequences, temporal and eternal.

> Evil consists essentially in the choice of what is lower in preference to what is higher...adultery instead of lawful procreation; slander, insult and perjury instead of right speaking; murder, stealing, striking fellowmen, drunkenness and insatiable gluttony instead of righteousness. All of these are sins of the soul, and there is no cause of them, they are only the rejection of better things. ATHANASIUS[11]

CHAPTER FOUR
Food For thought Comments

4(a). Why is Satan called the "god" of this age (Jn 12:31, Eph 2:2)?

God created angels before He created man. One of the angels was more glorious than all. His name was Lucifer. Lucifer was close to God in Heaven and had much power and glory. He and all the angels also had the gift of free will. Pride and greed grew in Lucifer. He coveted God's supremacy and took issue with His divine plan. Gathering together other rebellious spirits, he tried to unseat God from His throne (Isa 14:12-17). But no one can win a battle against God. Lucifer and his cohorts (one-third of the celestial beings/Rev 12:4) were evicted from Heaven forever and relegated to earth, where God allows them a certain amount of power in order to test, strengthen and teach those who call themselves His people.

Lucifer became known as "the Adversary"—Satan. God allowed Satan to tempt Adam and Eve as a test of their love. He allows everyone given the gift of life to be similarly tested. Dealing with temptation teaches dependence on God. Through trial and tribulation we learn that only by turning to Him in obedience do we receive grace in the form of strength to resist and endure. As with physical exercise, persistence in this struggle provides strength to deal with the next onslaught.

> The Devil is indeed angered when cast forth from a human body; but much more so if he sees a soul freed from sin. For this is his greatest power, the spreading of sin. Because of this Christ died, that He might break this power...If you destroy sin you have broken the nerves of the Devil, you have bruised his head, you have destroyed his power, you have defeated his army, you have wrought a sign greater than all miracles.
>
> CHRYSOSTOM[12]

The power that Satan has during this "age" of testing, though formidable, is vastly inferior to God's power. As the book of Job reveals dramatically, in His strength as Creator and Ruler of the universe, God allows Satan only that power which ultimately results in good: the separating of the obedient from the disobedient, the true believer from the unbeliever (Mt 3:12).

4(b). What are the enticements of the world that can lead us away from God?

The very temptations the Devil set before Christ (Mt 4:1-11) are also those he uses to entice us. When Satan tempted Jesus to use His power as the Son of God to turn stones into bread, he was pointing to our tendency to put satisfaction of bodily appetites first in life, whether they be food, possessions, or pleasure. The lure to jump off the highest point of the temple to see if God would send angels to rescue His Son points to pride, our inclination to have such exalted opinions of ourselves that we make demands upon God, as the Hebrew people did in their wanderings through the desert (Ex 17:1-7). The temptation in which Satan tried to interest Jesus in the kingdoms of the world points to our propensity for making our own agenda, for creating our own kingdoms with our own rules. This is what caused Adam and Eve to disobey God rather than grow in fellowship with Him as He desired.

> The ancient enemy tempted the first man by gluttony, when he persuaded him to eat the forbidden fruit of the tree; by vainglory when he said, *you shall be as gods* (Gen 3:5); by avarice, when he said: *knowing good and evil*. For avarice is not solely the desire of money but also of pride of place, when dignity is sought without measure. By these means [Satan] laid low the first man; by the same means he was defeated by the Second Man [Jesus].
>
> GREGORY THE GREAT[13]

Jesus' responses did not question Satan's right to tempt Him. Rather, they illustrate the fact that God expects His people to try to resist all worldly distractions which would take their eyes from the heavenly Kingdom as their goal in life. Jesus was tempted by Satan as Adam and Eve were and as we are, but He remained without sin (Heb 4:15). He overcame all temptation so He could be the example and the strength of those who turn to Him when their eyes, ears and hearts are drawn away from God (Heb 2:18).

> God so deals with us that while making progress towards Him we shall not forget our weakness; and that tempted we recall it, so that in our progress we may understand what we are from divine favour, and in our temptation what we are of our own strength. And such temptation would indeed lead us wholly astray were we not protected from above. Yet it assails us, though it does not break us; it incites us, though it does not move us; it shakes us, but does not make us fall: that we may see that it is because of our own weakness we are shaken, because of divine grace we stand firm. GREGORY THE GREAT[14]

4(c). What assistance does the Church offer to help us stay on the road to the Kingdom?

The Church is the Body of Christ, left on earth to continue His work of salvation. To help us win the battle against Satan, the Church offers grace through the Sacraments, the spiritual disciplines of worship, prayer and fasting, and the fellowship of others involved in the same struggle. Christ's personal involvement in the Mysteries of the Church and with the spiritual disciplines of prayer and fasting leave a powerful legacy to emulate.

> Christ fasted that we may learn how great a good it is and how effective a shield against the Devil...He fasted not because He needed to, but to teach us...And that He might lay down the length of our Lenten fast, He fasted for forty days and forty nights...He did not prolong His fast beyond that of Moses and Elijah, lest His taking on of our flesh might seem a thing not to be believed.
> CHRYSOSTOM[15]

4(d). What qualities in those involved in the difficulties of life cause renewed faith in those around them? What qualities create doubt and fear in others?

When those who suffer through no fault of their own turn to God for strength and courage and show their dependence upon Him without bitterness, they help others around them realize that there is indeed a powerful God Who loves and helps His people. Such was the effect caused by believers in the early Church who accepted torture and often painful death rather than deny Christ.

On the other hand, when those who call themselves Christians mumble and complain when things do not go their way, when they quickly allow the pressures of the world to water down their obedience to the word of God, and when they turn away from Him in anger when faced with the very difficult times of life, they convey the message that being a Christian has no special meaning—makes no real difference.

> When God first created the rose, it was without thorns. Since then the thorn has been added to its beauty to help us know that sorrow is very near to pleasure and to remind us of our sin, which condemned the earth to produce thorns.
> BASIL[16]

God has not promised His people a life free of care. He has promised to help us through troubled times if we turn to Him and trust Him (Isa 51:12, Mt 28:20, 2 Cor 1:3-4). His ultimate promise is eternal life with Him in His Kingdom if judgment shows evidence of true faith through all that life brings.

> In that hour when we shall be separated from men and from the traffic of men, be to us, O Lord, a Giver of good things, bringing joy to our sadness. When we have gone forth from this world, may we behold, O Lord, clearly and in deed the power of Your aid. Pour Your peace into our hearts, and give Your rest to all our striving, that the darkness of that night may be to us as day.
> EPHRAEM THE SYRIAN[17]

CHAPTER FIVE

That Which Awaits us

BACKGROUND: In Chapter Four, Paul wrote about the breaking down of the *outward* man due to suffering endured for the sake of preaching the Gospel and the subsequent purification of the *inward* man through faith, hope and perseverance. Now his thoughts turn to that which gives him confidence to remain joyful in the midst of this difficult process.

5:1. For we know that if our earthly house, this tent, is destroyed, we have a building from God, a house not made with hands, eternal in the Heavens. The dangers inherent in preaching the Gospel continue. Therefore, Paul's suffering goes on and the possibility of death for refusing to deny Christ or forsake His work is ever present. Paul is confident, however, of the truth that his soul is immortal. If his earthly body ceases to function, an even better body awaits him.

Paul calls the body an *earthly house*. As a tentmaker, He compares it to a *tent*—a temporary home for the soul to abide in while on earth. After judgment at the Second Coming of Christ, he who has demonstrated faith and prepared himself for life in God's Kingdom will receive a new imperishable body, an incorruptible house for the soul to inhabit.

> If a jeweler should make in mosaic the form of an animal, and the stones should be scattered by time or by the man who made them, he may gather them together again, and may form them in the same way, and make the same form of an animal. Shall not God be able to collect again the decomposed members of the flesh and make the same body as was formerly produced by Him?
>
> JUSTIN THE MARTYR[1]

5:2. For in this we groan, earnestly desiring to be clothed with our habitation which is from Heaven... Paul looks forward to the heavenly house his soul will dwell in eternally. This will not be an entirely different body but "the same one made incorruptible."[2]

> Be tender, I beseech you, of this body, and understand that you will be raised from the dead, to be judged with this body. CYRIL OF JERUSALEM[3]

> Although you may say: The remains of the flesh itself do not exist anywhere: they may have been consumed by fire, or devoured by a wild beast. Know this: whatever is consumed is contained in the bowels of the earth, and from there, at the command of God, it can be brought forth. For even you, where no fire is visible, can take flint and steel and strike fire from stone. That, therefore, which you do by effort and the skill God Himself has given you, so that you bring forth what is not visible, cannot the Divine Majesty do of His power? Believe me, God can do anything. CHRYSOSTOM[4]

FOOD FOR THOUGHT: (a). What other indications does the Bible give that everyone will spend eternity in a body? (b)...that the immortal body of a believer will be much like the one possessed in life on earth but different, with unique spiritual qualities?

5:3. if indeed, having been clothed, we shall not be found naked. The only thing Paul is concerned about is that at Judgment he not be *found naked* of faith, so that the body he will receive at the Resurrection will be his eternal habitation in joy, not in agony (Mt 25:41-46).

> Although the body is dissolved at the appointed time, because of the primeval disobedience, it is placed in the crucible of the earth, to be recast again...to each body its own soul shall be restored...possessing in every respect the things pertaining to it: not bodies diverse from what they had been...but as they departed this life, in sins or in righteous actions: and such as they were, such shall they be clothed with upon resuming life; and such as they were in unbelief, such shall they be faithfully judged. IRENAEUS[5]

> Be of good cheer, but work, strive earnestly; for nothing shall be lost. Every prayer, every psalm you sing is

> recorded; every good deed, every fast is recorded; every marriage duly observed is recorded; continence kept for God's sake is recorded...for you shall rise clothed with your own sins, or else with your righteous deeds.
>
> CYRIL OF JERUSALEM[6]

FOOD FOR THOUGHT: (c). What will be the conditions of eternal life in God's Kingdom? (d). What will be the characteristics of the resurrected bodies of the righteous?...the unrighteous?

5:4. For we who are in this tent groan, being burdened, not because we want to be unclothed, but further clothed, that mortality may be swallowed up by life. God created Adam and Eve to live forever and gave them one commandment to follow. After they disobeyed, He clothed them in *tunics of skin* (Gen 3:21), the mortality that came to man as a consequence of his fall from grace.[7] Mortality is the "biological condition, subject to the necessity of death" which became "a new law of the existence of the earthly creation."[8] Life in a mortal body is burdensome, prone to many difficulties and restricted by limitations. Still, life is a great blessing. If we do not love life, why would we long to live eternally? All Christians who have even the most basic understanding of the awesome truth of salvation through Jesus Christ long not to be rid of their bodies but to be clothed again in the immortal bodies Adam and Eve enjoyed before they disobeyed.

> The transformation of the body takes place in this way: while it is mortal and corruptible, it becomes immortal and incorruptible, not after its own proper substance, but after the mighty working of the Lord, Who is able to invest the mortal with immortality, and the corruptible with incorruption. IRENAEUS[9]

After the Second Coming of Christ, believers will experience life unending and perfect, with no sickness, no sorrow, no tears, no pain, no death (Rev 21:4). The joyful moments we experience during life on earth are tastes of the perfect joy of God's Kingdom in its fullness. Because of these bits of ecstasy, we are usually very reluctant to give up this life, wanting more and more of the "good" it has to offer. This instinctive desire to live forever is assurance from God that eternal life is a reality. The moments of suffering and despair we experience are tastes of Hell. God allows these experiences so we can make our choice. If we remember that the difficult times of life are allowed by God as a part of the process which brings His people to the surface and which strengthens and purifies them for life with Him, we help Him turn evil back to the good of His creation.

> **FOOD FOR THOUGHT:** (e). There are those, like Jehovah's Witnesses, who believe there is no Hell (in the sense of a state or place of eternal agony). This false teaching can cause much harm and eternal suffering. How?

5:5. Now He Who has prepared us for this very thing is God, Who also has given us the Spirit as a guarantee. Eternal life in communion with God has been a part of His plan for man from the beginning. The Holy Spirit, present within from the time of our Chrismation, calls us to holiness. If we cooperate and make an effort to feed and nurture our souls as we do our bodies, we grow spiritually. As this process continues, we receive ever-increasing glimpses into the wonder and joy of the Kingdom, which begins in this present life. This has a liberating effect in our lives. Our burdens seem lighter, in spite of the corruption of the world. We become increasingly secure in knowledge of the reality of the spiritual world and begin to respond to all of creation with love.

> It might seem to men of the present day, who are ignorant of God's appointment, to be a thing incredible and impossible that any man could live eternally...yet the ancients of the Old Testament lived to seven hundred, eight hundred and nine hundred years of age. Their bodies kept pace with the protracted length of their days and participated in life as long as God willed that they should live....and those who were translated [Enoch and Elijah, who did not die] do live as a guarantee of the future length of days. IRENAEUS[10]

5:6. Therefore we are always confident, knowing that while we are at home in the body we are absent from the Lord. The early Christians faced continual persecution and the ever-present threat of death, which was often the consequence of refusing to deny their faith in Christ. Like them, Paul does not fear death. Those born again spiritually of water and the Spirit through Baptism and Chrismation (Jn 3:3-5), followed by a life of faith, can share his confidence that to leave this life is to join Christ in His Kingdom—so there is no need for fear.

> What are we doing, we men of little faith, who grieve and rebel should one of our dear ones depart to the Lord? What are we doing, we whose pilgrimage on this earth delights us more than to be restored to the presence of Christ? In very truth, this whole life of ours is but a journey through a strange land. For as pilgrims in this world, we have here no certain dwelling; we suffer, we sweat, walking by ways that are difficult and full of peril. Treachery awaits us on every side, from spiritual enemies and from bodily ones; on every side the winding paths of error are made ready. And though beset by such dangers, not only do we wish not to be set free of them, but we even weep and mourn as lost those who have been delivered. What has God given us through His Only-begotten, if we still fear the coming of death? Why glory in being born again of water and the Holy Spirit, when we are saddened at the thought of going forth from this world?
>
> CHRYSOSTOM[11]

After their disobedience, God evicted Adam and Eve from the perfect setting they had enjoyed and placed angels at the gate so they would no longer have access to the tree of life (Gen 3:22-23). They found themselves in the imperfect world in which we live, where the devil has reign and where they would face deterioration and death.

Death is harsh, but it is not the enemy we tend to think it is. Death saves us from having to live on interminably after quality of life is gone. If we had to face the dangers of this world with no end to the ravages of time on our minds and bodies, at some point (through illness, age, or harm inflicted upon us) we would reach a state beyond healing. Each of us would face certain agony with no respite until Christ returns. Horror would ensue. God allows a glimpse of this untenable situation: all we need do is visit a long term care facility for the very sick or very old to see that the alternative to death would be infinitely worse. Death sets limits to personal pain and suffering and prevents unending mushrooming of sin. The world would be intolerable if the evil characters of history were not contained by death.

> God, and here lies the whole mystery of the "tunics of skin," introduces a certain order at the very heart of disorder to avoid a total disintegration by evil. His beneficent will organizes and preserves the universe; His punishment is pedagogy: better that man dies, that is to say, be excluded from the tree of life, than that his monstrous condition be made eternal. His finitude itself would make repentance well up within him...[12]

In His wisdom, God also allows (does not cause) the conditions which sometimes bring illness and death to the young as well as the old. This fact discourages carelessness and indifference and reminds us to be vigilant about the state of our souls, whatever our age. Because of fallen human nature, if each of us were guaranteed a certain number of years of life, it is probable that the majority would spend the greater number of them not worrying about God and what He expects of us, thinking that there is plenty of time. Toward the end of those promised years, however, instead of then turning our attention to God, we would probably be too far from knowledge of Him to even consider (much less know how to find) Him. The habits of a lifetime are not easily changed. The Christ-like life we are called to live guides us in building virtuous habits (ascesis).

> The curse of death has never been a judgment of God. It was the punishment of a loving Father, not the obtuse anger of a tyrant. Its character was educative and restorative. It prevented the perpetuation of an estranged life, the apathetic induction into an anti-natural condition. It not only put a limit to the decomposition of our nature, but, by the anguish of finitude, helped man to become alive to his condition and turn to God. Similarly, the unjust will of Satan cannot function except through the just permission of God. Satan's choice was not only limited by the divine will but also used by it, as we see in the case of Job.[13]

Before Christ's death on the Cross, however, death also meant separation from God. Man was unable to overcome the effects of sin on his own. Christ's mission was to overthrow all of them, including death, and to make possible again the union of man with God.

> The mere fact of incarnation overcomes the first obstacle to this union: the separation of the two natures, that of man and that of God. Two other obstacles then remain, linked to the fallen condition of man: sin and death. The work of Christ is to vanquish them, to banish their necessity from the terrestrial cosmos. Not to overcome them without redress, for that would be to violate the very liberty that created them. But to make death harmless and sin curable by submission of God Himself to death and Hell. Thus the death of Christ removes, from between man and God, the obstacle of sin; and His Resurrection takes from death its "sting."[14]

The fact that true Christians do not fear death does not mean, however, that we should seek premature death in any way. Life is precious and belongs to God. Only He knows His intent for each person's time on earth.

> No one has the right to raise his hand against himself, or slay himself against the will of God, his Creator, or drive the soul from the dwelling place of the body. But when he is called, and when his neighbor is called, let him go cheerful and rejoicing, and let him rejoice with those who are going. For this is the sum total of Christian belief: to look for our true life after death; at the end of life, to look for its return. CHRYSOSTOM[15]

> **FOOD FOR THOUGHT:** (f). Christ taught the early Christians to live with the constant thought that He might return at any moment (Mt 24:36, 25:13; Lk 21:34-36; 1 Thess 5:1-2). Why? (g). What happens to the soul after death?

5:7. For we walk by faith, not by sight. Though we are united with Christ through Eucharist and can know Him through the truths of the Gospel and the grace of the Holy Spirit, we do not see

Him bodily as did those who lived when He walked on earth. To try to live by God's word daily, without having seen Christ, is a demonstration of faith which He acknowledged when He said, *Blessed are they who have not seen, yet have believed* (Jn 20:29).

5:8-9. We are confident, yes, well pleased rather to be absent from the body and to be present with the Lord. Therefore we make it our aim, whether present or absent, to be well pleasing to Him. Life on earth is precious, but those who have true faith know that to be with the Lord in His Kingdom is infinitely better. The important thing, therefore, is to live in a manner which is *well pleasing* to God, so as to be ready for death, whenever it comes.

> **FOOD FOR THOUGHT:** (h). How can we live in a way that pleases God?

5:10. For we must all appear before the judgment seat of Christ, that each one may receive the things done in the body, according to what he has done, whether good or bad. Some are attracted to the Kingdom because of God's promise of its unequaled joy and love. The attention of others, however, is gained only through the more powerful fear of suffering. In his desire to lead all to salvation, Paul gives the full picture: each of us will face judgment at the feet of Christ and will spend eternity in circumstances determined by whether or not our lives as a whole demonstrated faith. This fact does not call for a legalistic following of rules—like the works of the Mosaic Law which Paul wrote against, required to be followed exactly to show man he could not earn salvation (Eph 2:9). Rather, it calls for a continuous attempt at Theosis: growth in those works which are the facets of a Christ-like life (Eph 2:10) that demonstrate and solidify faith and bring others to Him (Jas 2:14-26).

Most Protestant denominations teach what is called salvation by "faith alone": the belief that those who profess faith in Christ are automatically "saved," with no qualifying works or actions required. According to this theory, those who pronounce themselves saved because of their acknowledgement of Christ as Savior are guaranteed entrance to Heaven. Scripture which points to judgment is considered to refer only to the unsaved or as a determination of placement in the Kingdom, with levels assigned according to the good or bad one has done. But this verse states that *all* must face judgment, and 2 Cor 5:11 implies fear. Is there to be punishment in Heaven? Isn't being in God's presence, at any level, a state of glory? The Psalmist wrote: *I would rather be a doorkeeper in the house of my God than dwell in the tents of wickedness* (Ps 84:10).

The doctrine of salvation by faith alone began as opposition to the emphasis on legalistic-type works (in the sense of earning points) which developed in the Roman Church, culminating in the sixteenth century with the selling of indulgences, which implied that one could buy (or work) one's way to the Kingdom. Martin Luther was a Roman Catholic Priest who protested this aberration. He insisted that only faith in Christ is necessary for salvation, with no requirement for works of any type. His concerns were justified, but his theology constituted a break in the crucial connection between professed faith and the essential elements of a Christ-like life. The teaching of the early Church (preserved in Orthodoxy) is that faith is indeed the single criteria for salvation, but faith must be proved by one's life (2 Cor 13:5) and will be judged by God.

Those who espouse the concept of salvation by faith alone hold that a person who believes in Christ will automatically lead a Christ-like life. Luther taught that this will happen naturally, "as a cow gives milk." The problem is that this gives the misleading impression of a guaranteed conclusion. It is true that one who really has zealous faith will seek the truth, attempt to follow it, and consequently grow in holiness through the grace of God. The crucial point, however, is that conscious personal effort is required and is part of God's plan not to force but to work only in cooperation with man. God meets faith-demonstrating effort with His divine grace. God's grace and man's efforts, together, produce synergistic supernatural growth in Christ's image, toward the holiness that pervades in God's presence. The faith alone philosophy turned its adherents away from the Roman Church because its mass, hierarchical priesthood, Sacraments, etc. were considered "works" with the motivation of achieving credit towards salvation. But Luther himself soon became so distressed at the laxity of behavior in church attendance, lifestyle, etc. that his teachings began to produce in many who professed faith, that he imposed harsh discipline. In modern days, salvation by faith alone, has become known as "instant salvation." It holds great appeal for the "lukewarm" (Rev 3:16), who may or may not be part of a church. It allows them to blissfully consider themselves Christians, content that because they orally profess Christ as Savior they are headed toward Heaven, in spite of the absence of an attempt at Christ-like living. Those who have been lulled into such complacency feel that enlightened thinking has liberated them from what they consider to be the old-fashioned, legalistic moral constraints of the Bible. To live in a manner unconcerned with spiritual growth and doing the work of the Lord, however, or to intentionally disobey His word shows lack of real faith. He who does only as he pleases shows faith in himself over and above anything else, including God.

For the spiritually lazy, Martin Luther's well-intentioned Protestant Reformation efforts at reform and renewal have degenerated into the simplistic catch-all theory: Jesus died for sinners, so nothing is required of us. This has contributed to the watering-down of Christ's Gospel (Rev 12:15) and helps Satan continue to do, through false teachings, that which he failed to do through persecution in the early Church (Rev 12:13): divide the faithful and lead as many as possible away from God, like sheep to slaughter.

5:11. Knowing, therefore, the terror of the Lord, we persuade men; but we are well-known to God, and I also trust are well-known in your consciences. Paul tries to awaken everyone he meets to the fact that the aftermath of judgment is eternal: blessed life with God or the torment of being far removed from Him. This man who always zealously allowed his faith to guide his actions knows he must continue in that vein (Phil 3:12) or face *the terror of the Lord*. He is also aware that he must be a good role model for others. This awareness of the example we set as Christians is very important. Everything we say and do—our actions, inactions and reactions—can influence, positively or negatively, those with whom we come in contact.

> He who lives a worthy life draws grace upon himself; and he who receives such grace receives that he may help others to amend their lives...The beauty of a good life can help others more than miracles. I mean by a good life, not simply fasting nor lying down in sackcloth and ashes but to despise riches, to have charity towards your neighbor, to give of your bread to the hungry, to control your anger, to seek not vainglory, and to turn from envy.
>
> CHRYSOSTOM[16]

5:12. For we do not commend ourselves again to you, but give you opportunity to glory on our behalf, that you may have something to answer those who glory in appearance and not in heart. Paul offers the example of his life as a guide to the type of struggle required of those whose hearts are set on God's Kingdom. This contrasts sharply with false teachers who boast about themselves and their ministries but who, in reality, are spiritually dead.

5:13. For if we are beside ourselves, it is for God; or if we are of sound mind, it is for you. Paul's exuberance leads his detractors to say that he is not of sound mind. He responds that what they have witnessed is the spiritual ecstacy which fills him because of his love for God. But whether he is in that state or in a state of sober reflection, his intent is to bring them the truth of God's promises. This brings to mind the fact that, in the jargon of the world, someone who is zealous for sports, music or other such interests is called a fan, but someone who is enthused about God and His Kingdom is likely to be called a fanatic.

5:14-15. For the love of Christ constrains us because we judge thus: that if One died for all, then all died; and He died for all, that those who live should live no longer for themselves but for Him Who died for them and rose again. Death came through sin (Gen 2:17). Everyone born to man after the fall inherits this consequence—and a sinful nature. Christ was born of Mary, a pious, obedient maiden who was freed of the consequences of Adam and Eve's disobedience when she consented to bear the Son of God in her womb. She conceived through the Holy Spirit—supranaturally—outside the natural laws of procreation and heredity. Thus Christ was born with no association with the sin of Adam and Eve. He lived a sin-free life, so did not deserve to die. Yet he willingly became the scapegoat for the sins of mankind (Lev 16:10,21). He passed through death, then rose on the third day to show us there is life after death. If we try to grow in our understanding of these truths and the all-encompassing love demonstrated by them, we will develop a growing love for Christ. This love will manifest itself in a willingness to stand apart from the selfish ways of the world, in which personal goals for success and pleasure dominate. We will choose, instead, to live for Him—to continue the work He left for us.

> If there is true Christian love in a man, let him carry out the precepts of Christ. Who can describe the constraining power of love for God? Who can adequately express its majesty and beauty? No tongue can tell the heights to which love can lift us. Love binds us fast to God. Love casts a veil over sins innumerable. There are no limits to love's endurance, no end to its patience. Love is without servility, as it is without arrogance. Love knows of no divisions, promotes no discord; all the works of love are done in perfect fellowship. It was in love that all God's chosen saints were made perfect; for without love nothing is pleasing to Him. It was in love that the Lord drew us to Himself; because of the love He bore us, our Lord Jesus Christ, at the will of God, gave His blood for us—His flesh for our flesh, His life for our lives.
>
> CLEMENT OF ROME[17]

5:16. Therefore, from now on, we regard no one according to the flesh. Even though we have known Christ according to the flesh, yet now we know Him thus no longer. Those who realize that Christ is the promised Messiah do not consider Him as just another man who lived and died. They know Him by His position in the Kingdom, at the right hand of God, waiting for those who belong to Him. Paul writes that we should regard those around us in our lives in similar fashion: according to the degree that they reflect the image of Christ rather than the degree of worldly status they have attained. This was the attitude of Christ Himself, Who emphasized spiritual relationships above worldly when He said, *My mother and my brothers are [those] who hear the word of God and do it* (Lk 8:21).

> Let us beg and implore of God's mercy that we may be purged of all earthly preferences for this man or that, and be found faultless in love. Though every generation from Adam to the present day has passed from the earth, yet such of them as by God's grace were perfected in love have their place now in the courts of the godly, and at the visitation of Christ's Kingdom they will be openly revealed. For it is written, *Go into your secret chambers for a very little while, till my rage and fury pass away; and then I will remember a day of gladness, and raise you out of your graves.* CLEMENT OF ROME[18]

5:17. Therefore, if anyone is in Christ, he is a new creation; old things have passed away; behold, all things have become new. The oppressive Law of the Old Testament covenant has been fulfilled by the liberating force of Christ's sacrifice. To those who belong to Christ through Baptism, nothing is as it was before.

> Behold, both a new soul (for it was cleansed), and a new body, and a new worship, and promises new, and covenant, and life, and table and dress, and all things new absolutely. For instead of the Jerusalem below we have received that mother city which is above (Gal 4:26); and instead of a material temple have seen a spiritual temple; instead of tables of stone, fleshy ones; instead of circumcision, baptism; instead of manna, the Lord's Body; instead of water from a rock, blood from His side; instead of Moses' or Aaron's rod, the Cross; instead of the promised land, the Kingdom of Heaven; instead of a thousand priests, one High Priest; instead of a lamb without reason, a Spiritual Lamb. With these and such like things in his thought he said, *all things are new*. But *all* these *things are of God*, by Christ, and His free gift.
> CHRYSOSTOM[19]

5:18-19. Now all things are of God, Who has reconciled us to Himself through Jesus Christ and has given us the ministry of reconciliation, that is, that God was in Christ reconciling the world to Himself, not imputing their trespasses to them, and has committed to us the word of reconciliation. Through Christ, the second person of the Holy Trinity, in fulfillment of the first prophesy (see Gen 3:15 and this study for 1 Cor 2:6-8), God gave man the way back to union with Him—that which Adam and Eve lost for themselves and mankind when they disobeyed. This truth was given to the Apostles. All who continue their work of teaching the Gospel, whether clergy or laity, carry on Christ's ministry of reconciliation.

> Through Chrismation every member of the Church becomes a prophet and receives a share in the royal priesthood of Christ; all Christians alike, because they are chrismated, are called to act as conscious witnesses to the Truth. *You have an anointing (chrisma) from the Holy One, and know all things* (1 Jn 2:20).[20]

5:20-21. Therefore we are ambassadors for Christ, as though God were pleading through us: we implore you on Christ's behalf, be reconciled to God. For He made Him Who knew no sin to be sin for us, that we might become the righteousness of God in Him. An ambassador represents the leader of his country in a foreign land. He must speak the language and take part in the ways of that land but is a citizen of his own country. So too, true Christians are in the world, but not of it, *For our citizenship is in Heaven* (Phil 3:20).

> Christians have a unique citizenship of their own. They are, of course, citizens of their own lands—loyal ones too. Yet they feel like visitors. Every foreign country is their homeland, and their homeland is like a foreign country to them.
> MATHETES[21]

As Christ's ambassador, Paul urgently pleads that we all come to full realization of that which our Savior has done for us. Jesus not only accepted death undeservedly on our behalf, He also endured the indignities of crucifixion, the most dreaded torture (Gal 3:13). By humbling Himself to the utmost, Christ attained the highest glory (Phil 2:8-11). He promises that if we acknowledge Him as Savior and try to live according to His teachings, we take part in His righteousness. As a part of Him through Baptism, Eucharist, and a life of faith, we are no longer bound by the consequences of sin, so will share His glory.

> "God made Himself man, that man might become God." These powerful words, which we find for the first time in St. Irenaeus, are again found in the writings of St. Athanasius, St. Gregory of Nazianzus, and St. Gregory of Nyssa. The Fathers and Orthodox theologians have repeated them in every century with the same emphasis, wishing to sum up in this striking sentence the very essence of Christianity: an ineffable descent of God to the ultimate limit of our fallen human condition, even unto death—a descent of God which opens to men a path of ascent, the unlimited vistas of the union of created beings with the Divinity.[22]

We find it easy to remember that God took on flesh and died to redeem us from sin, but we also easily forget the reason: that we "might become God." Consequently, too often our glorious potential remains unrealized. We can become God to the extent that we grow in union with Him, but that which man can know of God, and partake of, is not His divine essence, but His "operations" or "energies."

> We know our God from His operations, but do not undertake to approach near to His essence. His operations come down to us, but His essence remains beyond our reach.
> BASIL[23]

God's essence is often compared to the solar disk and His energies to its rays.[24] We can see the light which emanates from the sun and can feel its heat but cannot approach the source or gaze upon its brilliance directly, even from a great distance. So it is with God. We can partake of that which flows from Him but not of that which makes Him God—for He is unknowable, inaccessible. "We are created beings, called to become by grace what God is by His nature. If one could participate in the essence itself, God would no longer be Trinity, but a multitude of persons."[25]

Those who grow in holiness do so because they partake of (plug-in to) the actual energies of God. We avail ourselves of those energies by disciplining our will to follow His bidding. To the extent we do so, we actually take on His qualities, as an object added to a glowing fire takes on the characteristics of fire.

> This is why the saints are the instruments of the Holy Spirit, having received the same energy He has.
>
> GREGORY PALAMAS[26]

It is through these energies of God that man is divinely activated and can actually have a direct relationship with God during his earthly life and beyond. Bishop Kallistos Ware writes: "In relation to man, the divine energy is in fact nothing else than the grace of God."[27] Man has access to God's grace, His energies, through the operations of each of the three persons of the Godhead.

> The Father, the Son and the Holy Spirit alike hallow, quicken, enlighten and comfort. No one will attribute a special and peculiar operation of hallowing to the operation of the Spirit after hearing the Savior in the Gospel saying to the Father about His disciples, "Sanctify them by your Truth" (Jn 17:11,17). In like manner all other operations are equally performed, in all who are worthy of them, by the Father and by the Son and by the Holy Spirit; every grace and virtue, guidance, life, consolation, change into the immortal, the passage into freedom and all other good things which come down to man.
>
> BASIL[28]

CHAPTER FIVE
Food For Thought Comments

5(a). What indications does the Bible give that everyone, believers as well as non-believers, will live eternally in a body?

FROM THE OLD TESTAMENT:

For I know that my Redeemer lives, and He shall stand at last on the earth; and after my skin is destroyed, this I know, that ***in my flesh*** *I shall see God* (Job 19:25-26). Job clearly foretells Christ the Redeemer...speaking not of "my Creator," but of *my Redeemer*...But tell us clearly I beg you, Blessed Job, what you believe, concerning the resurrection of your own flesh....I ask to learn the manner of this resurrection. For I believe that I shall rise again, but I desire to know of what nature shall I be? For I must know whether I shall rise again in some other subtle or perhaps ethereal body or in this body in which I die. For if I rise again in another, ethereal body, it will no longer be I who shall rise. For how can that be a true resurrection, if there cannot be a true body? Plain reason tells me that if the body is not true, then beyond doubt there shall be no true resurrection. Nor can it be rightly called a resurrection, when that does not rise which died. O Blessed Job, take from us these clouds of doubt, and as you, through the grace of the Holy Spirit, have already begun to speak to us of our hope of resurrection, make clear to us if our flesh shall truly rise again. There follows: *in my flesh I shall see God*.

GREGORY THE GREAT[29]

Your dead shall live; Together with my dead body they shall arise. Awake and sing, you who dwell in dust; For your dew is like the dew of herbs, and the earth shall cast out the dead (Is 26:19). Perhaps you fear that your dry bones cannot be clothed again in their former flesh? Do not measure the power of God by your own weakness. God, the Creator of all things, Who clothes the trees with leaves, the fields with flowers, can also, at the Resurrection, clothe your bones with their true flesh. Ezekiel the prophet on one occasion doubted this very thing, and asked by the Lord whether the dry bones he saw scattered over the plain would live again, replied: *Oh Lord God, You know* (Ez 37:3). But after the Lord commanded him to prophesy concerning these bones, he saw the bones come together, each one to its joint, and when he had seen the dry bones bound together with sinew and interwoven with veins and covered with flesh and the skin stretched out over them he prophesied in the spirit, and the spirit of each one entered into the bodies lying there, and they rose from the dead, and directly they *stood upon their feet*. And the prophet, reassured in this way of the truth of the resurrection of the dead, wrote down the vision, that those who came after him might come to know of this wondrous happening. CHRYSOSTOM[30]

FROM THE NEW TESTAMENT:

Behold My hands and My feet, that it is I Myself. Handle Me and see, for a spirit does not have flesh and bones as you see I have (Lk 24:39). When I was living in the city of Constantinople at the time of this Eutychius (who once said our future bodies would be impalpable and more ethereal than air), I put this testimony from the Gospel to the truth of our resurrection before him. He replied: "The Lord did this to remove all doubt of His Resurrection from the hearts of His Disciples." To this I said: "This is truly an extraordinary thing you are saying: that doubt should arise in us from the same grounds which took away all doubts from the hearts of the Disciples?" If you assert that He did not possess that which He showed them, which confirmed the faith of His Disciples, then our faith is destroyed. He then went on to say that the Lord had the palpable Body He showed them. But after He had confirmed the hearts of those who touched Him, all that could be touched in the Lord was then reduced to a certain subtlety. To this I answered: "It is written that Christ, rising again from the dead, dies now no more; Death shall no more have dominion over Him" (Rom 6:9). If, therefore, after His Resurrection anything of His Body could suffer change, contrary to the truth of what Paul has said, then after His Resurrection the Lord returned to death. And what person however foolish would say this, except one who denies the true Resurrection of His Body?

To this he objected, saying to me: "Since it is written that...*flesh and blood cannot possess the Kingdom of God* (I Cor 15:50), on what ground can we believe that the body shall truly rise again?" To this I replied "In Sacred Writ flesh is spoken of in one way in regard to its nature, in another in regard to its guilt or corruption. Of flesh as nature it was written: *This now is bone of my bones, and flesh of my flesh (Gen 2:23); and The Word was made flesh and dwelt among us* (Jn 1:14). Of flesh as guilt it was written: *My spirit shall not remain in man forever because he is flesh* (Gen 6:3). And the Psalmist says: *and he remembers that they are flesh: a breath that passes away and does not come again* (Ps 78:39). And it was in this sense Paul said to the disciples: *You are not in the flesh, but in the spirit* (Rom 8:9). It was not that the persons to whom he was writing were no longer in the body, but that they had mastered the impulses of the body's desires; and being now free through the power of the Spirit, were no longer *in the flesh*.

Accordingly, Paul saying that *flesh and blood cannot possess the Kingdom of God* means that flesh here stands for guilt, not for our nature. For in his next words he shows he was speaking of flesh as guilt when he adds: *Neither shall corruption possess incorruption*. Therefore flesh shall be in the glory of that Heavenly Kingdom, in its nature, but *not in the passion of lust*; and the sting of death overcome, it shall reign incorrupt forever..."

Going on with this question for a long time, we began to feel a great resentment towards one another. Then the Emperor, Constantine Tiberius of pious memory, received us both in private to learn of the disagreement between us. After weighing the written presentation of the case by either side, he decided that the book Eutychius had written on the Resurrection should be committed to the flames. Upon leaving, I became very ill, and the same happened to Eutychius, who died a little later. At the time of his death, as there was almost no one who followed his teaching, I dropped the prosecution of it, lest I should appear to be shooting arrows at his ashes. But while he was still alive, and while I was ill with fever, to those I knew who went to visit him he would say, holding

> the skin of his hand before their eyes: "I confess that in this flesh we shall all rise again." And this, they tell me, he used to deny totally. GREGORY THE GREAT[31]

5(b). What indications does the Bible give that, after the Resurrection, the immortal body of a believer will be much like that possessed in life on earth but different, with unique spiritual qualities?

The references to Jesus after His Resurrection indicate that though those who had known Him before His death were able to recognize Him, not all did so immediately. This was due to the fact that they were not expecting to see Him alive again, and because at His Resurrection His body was made incorruptible, which made His appearance similar yet different.

Mt. 28:1-10: This account shows that the women recognized Jesus, thus His post-Resurrection appearance must have been similar to His pre-Resurrection appearance.

Jn 20:11-18: Mary, however, recognized Jesus only after He spoke her name, a sound familiar to her ears, indicating that there was something different about His physical appearance.

Jn 20:19: When the doors were shut, Jesus came and stood in their midst. The special qualities of His resurrected body enabled Him to be present in a room without entering through a door or window.

Lk 24:13-31: When two of the (seventy) disciples were on the road to Emmaus, Jesus drew near and began to walk with them. They did not recognize Him, however, until He blessed bread, broke it and gave it to them, something they had seen Him do before (Mt 14:19; 26:26). Then He *vanished from their sight*, another indication of the special qualities of His resurrected body.

The body in which we spend eternity will be a "spiritual body." Bishop Kallistos Ware wrote: "This does not mean that at the Resurrection our bodies will be somehow dematerialized; but we are to remember that matter as we know it in this fallen world, with all its inertness and opacity, does not at all correspond to matter as God intended it to be. Freed from the grossness of the fallen flesh, the resurrection body will share in the qualities of Christ's human body at the Transfiguration and after the Resurrection. But, although transformed, our resurrection body will still be in a recognizable way the same body as that which we have now: there will be continuity between the two."[32]

> After our future resurrection, our flesh shall be the same and different: the same in nature, different through glory; the same in its reality, different in its power. It shall indeed be subtle because it shall be incorruptible. It shall be palpable because it shall not lose the essence of its true nature. GREGORY THE GREAT[33]

> For it is just that in the body in which the righteous toiled or were afflicted, being proved in every way by suffering, they should receive the reward of their suffering; and that in the body in which they were slain because of their love for God, in that they should be revived again; and that in the body in which they endured servitude, in that they should reign. For God is rich in all things, and all things are His. It is fitting, therefore, that the creation itself [the body], being restored to its primeval condition, should without restraint be under the dominion of the righteous. IRENAEUS[34]

5(c). What will be the conditions of eternal life in God's Kingdom?

Perfection is dynamic, not static. The righteous will rise in perfect, immortal bodies and will continually grow in union with God.

> For if on earth Jesus Christ healed the sicknesses of the flesh and made the body whole, much more will He do this in the Resurrection, so that the flesh shall rise perfect and entire, with all dreaded difficulties healed.
> JUSTIN THE MARTYR[35]

> Godliness is perfection that is never complete.
> PHILOTHEOS OF SINAI[36]

There shall be no marrying, to beget children. For there shall be no death; nor growing up, because no one grows old. There shall be no eating, for there shall be no hunger. (The power to eat and to drink shall remain after the Resurrection, as it did with Christ, but not the need...[37]) There shall be no buying or selling, for there shall be no want...The Sabbath (day of rest) shall be unbroken: what the Jews celebrate for a period of time, we shall celebrate for all eternity.

There shall be ineffable rest...for as we are born in the body to toil, we are reborn in the spirit to rest; ...Here He feeds us, there He perfects us; here He promises, there He shall give; here He foretells, there He shall show us the reality. And when we are safe and perfected, in spirit and in body, within that blessedness, the things of this world shall be no more;

...but we shall not sleep in idleness; for sleep itself is now given to us as refreshment for the weariness of the soul. For the fragile body cannot endure the unceasing striving that agitates our mortal senses, unless this fragility is renewed, through the sleep of the senses, to enable it to bear this agitation. And as the renewal to come shall be from death, so is waking now from sleep. Therefore there shall be no sleep. For where there is no death, there shall be no image of death.

All our activity shall be, "Amen" and "Alleluia"...Do not be saddened by thinking, in earthly fashion, that if one of you were to stand every day saying, "Amen" and "Alleluia," he would soon wither away from sheer tedium, if he did not fall asleep from repetition and long for silence; and from this go on to think of that life as unpleasing and undesirable...We shall say "Amen" and "Alleluia," not in sounds that come and go, but with the love of our soul...Amen means "so be it"; alleluia, "praise God"... Because we shall, with unceasing delight, see Truth there, and contemplate it in shining clarity. Inflamed with the love of this Truth and clinging to it in sweet, chaste, and incorporeal embrace, we shall praise it and say "Alleluia." Exhorting each other to the same praise, and with most ardent charity towards one another and towards God, all who are citizens of that City shall sing, "Alleluia"; as they shall say "Amen."

AUGUSTINE[38]

5(d). What will be the characteristics of the resurrected bodies of the righteous?...of the unrighteous?

The resurrected bodies of both the righteous and the unrighteous will be immortal—but they will be decidedly different.

> If a man is righteous, he will receive a heavenly body, that he may be able to converse with angels; but if a man is a sinner, he shall receive an eternal body fit to endure the penalties of sins. And righteously will God assign either state, for we do nothing without the body. We blaspheme with the body, and with the mouth we pray. With the body we commit fornication, and with the body we keep chastity. With the hand we rob, and by the hand we bestow alms; and the rest in like manner. Since then the body has been our minister in all things, it shall also share with us in the future the fruits of the past.
>
> CYRIL OF JERUSALEM[39]

> The bodies of the impious shall be unchanged; nothing shall appear to be taken from them. But their unchanged body shall be for a punishment; and this sort of consistency, if I may call it so, is a corruptible consistency. For where there is pain there is corruption: and the former liability to pain shall not cease, pain itself shall not die. For we believe that this corruption was referred to prophetically by the term *worm*, and pain, by the word *fire*. But since this consistency shall be such that it shall neither yield to death through pain nor be changed to that incorruption in which there is no pain, for this reason was it written: *Their worm shall not die, and their fire shall not be quenched* (Is 66:24; Mk 9:43-48).
>
> AUGUSTINE[40]

> Well! I know what a chill comes over you on hearing these things; but what am I to do? This is God's own command, to continually tell you these truths.
>
> CHRYSOSTOM[41]

5(e). There are those, like Jehovah's Witnesses, who believe that there is no Hell (in the sense of a state or place of eternal agony). This false teaching can cause much harm and eternal suffering. How?

Jehovah's Witnesses profess that, ultimately, the unrighteous will be totally annihilated. This false teaching is very attractive to many and inspires the saying: *Let us eat, drink and be merry, for tomorrow we die* (Is 22:13). The Devil wants us to believe that there is no Hell for the same reason he would like us to believe that he does not exist. If we are unaware of his presence, we will be unaware of the traps he sets for us—the ways in which he tries to lead us away from God. Those who believe there is no Hell may choose to spend their lives following their own will instead of trying to determine and discipline themselves according to God's will, content with what they think will be a blissful future of non-existence. In either case, Satan will have attained his goal of diverting many from the Kingdom.

It will literally be a rude awakening, to those who succumb to the comforts of this heresy and squander their lives with no concern for the obedience and spiritual growth God expects, to find not merciful oblivion but eternal agony: *the worm that does not die* and the *fire that is not quenched* (Mk 9:48): an awful, never-ending painful realization of having denied oneself blessedness and eternal joy.

5(f). Christ taught the early Christians to live with the constant thought that He might return at any moment (Mt 24:36, 25:13; Lk 21:34-36; 1 Thess 5:1-2). Why?

For the same reason that God does not want us to know the length of our individual lives. He wants us to live in a state of readiness so we do not become negligent about our relationship with Him. Death can come upon us unexpectedly, as can Christ's Second Coming. Either event marks the end of our opportunity to demonstrate our faith and to grow in holiness in preparation for the Kingdom. Both are times of judgment. Therefore, each day of our lives we must try to grow in Christ's image so that we are always ready to meet our Lord.

5(g). What happens to the soul after death?

After death, the soul leaves the body and lives on because it is immortal. Partial judgment takes place. In its unending existence, the soul enters a new state in which it "presenses and foretastes, to a certain degree, that which it shall experience in full after the Second Coming of Christ and final judgment. The soul of the righteous foretastes and experiences the beneficences of Heaven and Paradise....The soul of the sinner foretastes and experiences the fearful sufferings of Hell."[42] When we sleep we experience a foreshadowing of this state of existence between death of the earthly body and the resurrected state after the Second Coming of Christ: though our body is immobile, through dreams we may participate in many experiences.

> When the body lies in bed, not moving but in death-like sleep, the soul keeps awake by virtue of its own power. It transcends the natural power of the body and as though traveling away from the body while remaining in it, imagines and beholds things above the earth. Often it even holds converse with the saints and angels who are above earthly and bodily existence and approaches them in the confidence of the purity of its intelligence. Shall it not all the more, when separated from the body at the time appointed by God Who coupled them together, have its knowledge of immortality more clear? For if even when coupled with the body it lived a life outside the body, much more shall its life continue after the death of the body and live without ceasing by reason of God Who made it thus by His own Word, our Lord Jesus Christ.
>
> ATHANASIUS[43]

The resurrection of the dead will take place at the Second Coming of Christ, when "every soul shall unite itself to the body which it possessed during its life on earth...it will be a spiritual, not a material one. In this way we shall all appear before the tribunal of Christ."[44] After this final and complete judgment, each person will experience eternally, with both body and soul, that for which s/he has prepared. What the soul had become inwardly during life on earth will become evident outwardly in the body. We will be what we have practiced to be.

The glory that in the present life enriches the souls of the saints will cover and enfold their naked bodies at the Resurrection and will carry them to Heaven. Then with body and soul the saints will rest with God in the Kingdom forever. For God, when He created Adam, did not give him bodily wings as He gave to the birds: His purpose was to confer the wings of the Spirit on him at the Resurrection, so that he might be lifted up by them and carried wherever the Spirit desired. Such spiritual wings are given to the souls of the saints in this present life so that their understanding may be raised by them to the spiritual realm. For the world of the Christians is a different world, with different garments, different food and a different form of enjoyment. We know that when Christ comes from Heaven to resurrect all those who have died during the present age, He will divide them into two groups (Mt 25:31-33). Those who bear His sign, which is the seal of the Holy Spirit, He will set at His right hand, saying: *My sheep, when they hear My voice, recognize Me* (Jn 10:14). Then He will envelop their bodies with the divine glory that, through their good works and the Spirit, their souls have already received in this present life. MAKARIOS OF EGYPT[45]

5(h). How can we live in a way that pleases God?

If, every time we must make an important decision, we try to determine what God asks of us and do our best to act accordingly, we will grow in the image of Christ and thus will please God.

Wear a garment of incorruption, resplendent in good works; and whatever matter you receive from God to administer as a steward, administer profitably. Have you been given riches? Dispense them well. Have you been entrusted with the word of teaching? Be a good steward thereof. Have you power to rule? Do this diligently. There are many doors of good stewardship. Only let none of us be condemned and cast out; that we may with boldness meet Christ, the everlasting King, who reigns forever. CYRIL OF JERUSALEM[46]

If you have the fire of lust, set against it that other fire (Mt 13:42), and this will presently be quenched and gone. If you wish to utter some harsh sounding words, think of the gnashing of teeth, and the fear will be a bridle to your tongue. If you wish to plunder, hear the Judge commanding, *Bind him hand and foot, and cast him into the outer darkness* (Mt 22:13), and you will cast out this lust also. If you are drunken, and overindulge continually, hear the rich man saying, *Send Lazarus, that with the tip of his finger he may cool this scorching tongue* (Lk 16:24), yet not obtaining this, and you will hold yourself aloof from that distemper. If you love luxury, think of the affliction there, and you will not think at all of this. If you are harsh and cruel, think of those virgins who when their lamps had gone out missed the bridal chamber (Mt 25:12), and you will quickly become humane. Are you sluggish, and remiss? Consider him who hid the talent (Mt 25:24-30), and you will be more vehement than fire. Are you devoured by desire of what belongs to your neighbor? Think of the worm that does not die, and you will easily both put away from you this disease, and in all other things act virtuously. He has asked of us nothing irksome or oppressive. Why then do His injunctions appear irksome to us? From our laziness. If we labor diligently, even what appears intolerable will be light and easy; but if we are lazy, even things tolerable will seem difficult. CHRYSOSTOM[47]

CHAPTER SIX
Through Whom God Works

BACKGROUND: As Chapter Five ended, Paul pleaded that his readers be reconciled to God by taking full advantage of the grace of Christ's saving work. He proceeds to warn about the perils of wasting grace.

6:1. We then, as workers together with Him, also plead with you not to receive the grace of God in vain. The grace of which Paul writes is the opportunity for salvation through Christ. He begs his readers not to waste this gift, which is available to everyone. God has offered knowledge of this grace to mankind through those who have continued Christ's work through the ages. Inspired authors of Scripture, Fathers of the Church whose writings preserve its intended meaning, priests, monks, theologians, teachers, parents and all who have really believed the Gospel have passed on the same urgent message: use life for its ultimate purpose—to learn about God's plan for those who would like to live eternally with Him and try to live accordingly in order to demonstrate faith and be rendered righteous (Mt 13: 41-43).

> So they won't think that *reconciliation* (5:18-19) comes from merely believing in Him Who calls, he adds these words, requiring that earnestness which respects the life....For from *grace* we reap no benefit towards salvation if we live impurely; no, we are even harmed, having greater aggravation of our sins, if after such knowledge and such a gift we go back to our former vices.
>
> CHRYSOSTOM[1]

6:2. For He says: "In an acceptable time I have heard you, and in the day of salvation I have helped you." Behold, now is the accepted time; behold, now is the day of salvation. Quoting Isaiah 49:8, Paul relates that God helps us to fulfill life's potential of union with Him by reaching out to each of us in *an acceptable time:* our lifetime—the time allotted to ponder and pursue salvation. We never know when this life and, therefore, this opportunity will end through death or the Second Coming of Christ, so the present day is the only one of which we can be certain. It is therefore *the day of salvation*: our chance to consciously commit or recommit our lives to Christ—tomorrow may be too late.

> **FOOD FOR THOUGHT:** (a). What regular reminders are Orthodox Christians given of the need to commit or recommit their lives to Christ continually?

6:3. We give no offense in anything, that our ministry may not be blamed. Paul does not allow himself any personal leeway. He strives to be a good example of the Christian life in all ways so those observing his way of life will have no cause to reject the Gospel on his account. This is a verse that anyone in the position of influencing others by his example would do well to memorize.

6:4-5. But in all things we commend ourselves as ministers of God: in much patience, in tribulations, in needs, in distresses, in stripes, in imprisonments, in tumults, in labors, in sleeplessness, in fastings; In carrying out the work God set before him, Paul not only patiently endures but triumphs over those external trials and tribulations his work and the enemies of the Gospel bring. Though often without adequate food and sleep, he also willingly participates in the discipline of fasting for the spiritual strength it affords, so he will be able to continue the struggle.

On a personal level regarding salvation, there is no exemption from spiritual growth and struggle for those who are God's ministers. All Christians are required to try to live the life as well as teach it to others.

> *Obey those who rule over you, and be submissive, for they watch out for your souls, as those who must give account* (Heb 13:17).

> ...but neither he who pursues political rule nor he who pursues spiritual rule will be able to administer it unless he has first ruled himself as he ought.
>
> CHRYSOSTOM[2]

6:6. by purity, by knowledge, by long-suffering, by kindness, by the Holy Spirit, by sincere love ...These are fruits of the Holy Spirit, the gifts with which God meets man's efforts at spiritual growth (see Gal 5:22-24). The fact that Paul possesses these gifts shows that he is a true teacher of God's word.

> Paul received grace, but he himself was the cause who by his good works and his toils attracted grace. And ...he also did not misuse the gifts of the Spirit.
>
> CHRYSOSTOM[3]

FOOD FOR THOUGHT: (b). How can the gifts of the Spirit be misused?

6:7. by the word of truth, by the power of God, by the armor of righteousness on the right hand and on the left; The power of God is available through the Sacraments of the Church, which are vehicles of grace. Paul's effectiveness in his ministry stems from acting according to God's will, by which he clothes himself in the armor of righteousness. This advantage is accessible to all who develop, teach and live by an understanding of the fullness of the truths preserved by the early Church (read Eph 6:11-18).

> "But," you say, "virtue is burdensome and distasteful, while with vice, great pleasure is blended; and the one is wide and broad, but the other straight and narrow."...Suppose there were two roads, one leading to a furnace, and the other to a Paradise; and the one to the furnace was broad, while the other to Paradise, narrow. Which road would you take? CHRYSOSTOM[4]

6:8-10. by honor and dishonor, by evil report and good report; as deceivers, and yet true; as unknown, and yet well known; as dying, and behold we live; as chastened, and yet not killed; as sorrowful, yet always rejoicing; as poor, yet making many rich; as having nothing, and yet possessing

all things. Paul dealt with the extremes of life, as do all who sincerely try to live and teach the fullness of the Gospel. He was honored by some, dishonored by others.

> ...when the teachers are held in honor, many are inspired to godliness. And besides, this is a proof of good works, and glorifies God. CHRYSOSTOM[5]

To receive *honor* is very pleasant, but it presents a particular danger to the recipient. It is difficult to accept praise humbly, in a Christ-like manner, and sincerely give all glory to God. The sin of pride can easily rear its ugly head.

> God is opposed to nothing so much as to pride. And because of this there is nothing He has not done, since the beginning, to overthrow this evil disposition. Because of it we are subject to death and live in grief and pain; because of it we labor in sweat, in toil and in afflictions without end.
>
> Through pride, the first man sinned because he aspired to become equal to God and so did not even keep what he already had, but fell from everything. For it is the nature of pride that not only does it add nothing to our life, it also takes from us that which we have. Humility takes nothing from us but rather adds what we do not have.
> CHRYSOSTOM[6]

FOOD FOR THOUGHT: (c). What are the signs of pride?

The antidote to the spiritual danger posed by the poison of excessive honor and praise, especially to those who try to teach the Gospel, is to remember that no one can share credit for the only thing that has eternal value: God's divine plan for our salvation through Christ. It was instituted by God, executed by Christ, and empowered by the Holy Spirit. The greatest Apostles, preachers and teachers have felt awed, humbled and unspeakably grateful to be allowed a role in bringing knowledge and understanding of it to others. It was in this spirit that John the Baptist, whom Jesus called the greatest man to have lived, proclaimed that he was not even worthy to untie Christ's sandals (Mk 1:7).

The true Christian walks against the winds of the world most of the time, so struggle is part of the course. Along the way there are always those who do not want to hear God's truths because they do not want to have to change their lives accordingly. Their reaction may be to try to discredit the messenger so they can feel justified in ignoring the message. Paul often faced such *dishonor*. When he did, he tried to take that also in stride, following Christ's example. Accepting dishonor when it comes is the balance to accepting honor and staves off vainglory.

> The first step in overcoming vainglory is to remain silent and to accept dishonor gladly. The middle stage is to check every act of vainglory while it is still in thought. The end—insofar as one may talk of an end to an abyss—is to be able to accept humiliation before others without actually feeling it. CLIMACUS[7]

Some have *good* things to say about Paul, and some *evil*. Some say he *deceives* those to whom he preaches, and others say his teachings are *true* to the word of God. In facing both extremes, he endeavors to respond as Christ would. To some he is *unknown*, no one important; to others he is *well-known*, and has changed many lives. Some dismiss him and the power God wielded through him because they think he is *dying*. They know he is under the constant threat of death and feel he won't be around long, yet he continues to *live* and work and bring people to God, *as chastened and yet not killed*. He is often *sorrowful* because of the ungodly conditions of the world which imperil his ministry and his life, yet he is *always rejoicing* because he knows the certainty of eternal life with God in His Kingdom for those who endure to the end (Mt 10:22).

The Apostles were *poor* in worldly possessions yet rich spiritually and *made many rich* in that which really matters—knowledge of Christ. In addition, however, the riches of the world were available to them to partake of through those they taught. Because they were willing to trust God and spent their time and energy storing up spiritual rather than material treasures, they lived *as having nothing, yet possessing all things*. Paul experienced both extremes of human emotion: from enemies of the Gospel, hatred and abuse but from friends of the Gospel, great love and generosity; some of whom, he wrote, would gladly pluck out their own eyes to give to him (Gal 4:15).

> He who gives temporal aid to those who have spiritual gifts to bestow is a cooperator in spiritual giving. For since there are few who possess spiritual gifts and many who abound in temporal things, through this means they who have possessions partake in the virtues of those who are needy by relieving from their own abundance the wants of these sanctified poor.
> GREGORY THE GREAT[8]

> Some say that spiritual riches are spoken of here; but I would say that the carnal are too; for they were rich in these also, having, after a new kind of manner, the houses of all opened to them. CHRYSOSTOM[9]

FOOD FOR THOUGHT: (d). This brings to mind Jesus' words: *Seek first the Kingdom of God and His righteousness, and all things shall be added to you* (Mt 6:33). How can this principle be applied to our modern lives?

6:11-12. O Corinthians! We have spoken openly to you, our heart is wide open. You are not restricted by us, but you are restricted by your own affections. The Greek text means more literally "...our heart is enlarged." A heart that feels love seems to expand; it has room for more. The one who loves showers his beloved with tokens of affection. Because of the love Paul feels for the people of Corinth, his words are filled with great emotion. There is no limit to his love for them (2 Cor 12:15), therefore, no limit to the lengths he will go to make them understand the word of God. However, they are limited in their response to the Christian life by the depth of their love for him and for God. As a person's love grows, commitment to a Christ-like life to show this love will deepen.

> He who loves the Lord has first loved his brother, for the latter is proof of the former. CLIMACUS[10]

> If you love God, you will be an imitator of His kindness.
> MATHETES[11]

> It is for love's sake that he who is in a state of obedience obeys what is commanded. Good works are done out of love for one's neighbor; while vigils, psalmody, and the like are done out of love for God.
>
> PETER OF DAMASKOS[12]

6:13. Now in return for the same (I speak as to children), you also be open. He asks for their love in return—that their hearts expand to include love for him and that which he is trying to teach. Since he was the first to bring the Gospel to the Corinthians, he speaks as a spiritual father to his children, who should respond to his sacrificial love for them.

6:14-15. Do not be unequally yoked together with unbelievers. For what fellowship has righteousness with lawlessness? And what communion has light with darkness? And what accord has Christ with Belial? Or what part has a believer with an unbeliever? To "yoke" is to join together. Paul does not say that we should not associate with unbelievers (1 Cor 10:27), for then no outreach would be possible. Rather, he writes that believers should not be joined together or closely united with unbelievers, as the Mosaic Law stated that an ox should not be yoked with a donkey in plowing (Deut 22:10) because they cannot work well together to accomplish the task at hand. In Paul's time, Christianity was new and all were converts to it, so many of the early Christians had spouses and/or other family members outside the faith. Christians were not to leave their non-Christian spouses (1 Cor 7:12), but an unmarried Christian was expected to refrain from marrying an unbeliever (1 Cor 7:39) because to do so might create conflict and cause a diminishment of the believer's commitment to a Christ-like life.

The story told in Acts 16:16-18 suggests also that a Christian should not be yoked with an unbeliever in doing any form of God's work. When the evil spirit in the slave girl began to join in Paul's work by testifying as to the truth of who he was, Paul would not allow that cooperation, to prevent the evil spirit from using the association to gain people's confidence and then lead them away from God. Not all voices speaking about God are godly. Some may try to use God's word for their own purposes (2 Cor 11:13-15).

Just as *righteousness* and *lawlessness*, *light* and *darkness* and *Christ and Belial* (Hebrew for Satan) are the complete opposite of each other, a *believer* is the complete opposite of an *unbeliever* in attitudes toward life and its purpose, so the two cannot be joined with good result. This is the basis for the Church's teaching that a Christian cannot be united in matrimony with a non-Christian and that, ideally, individuals contemplating marriage should be united, not divided, in faith so as to begin their lives together on a solid foundation—suitable for creating a family and guiding all members towards God.

6:16. And what agreement has the temple of God with idols? For you are the temple of the living God. As God has said: "I will dwell in them and walk among them. I will be their God, and they shall be My people." The Spirit of God dwells in those who are Baptized and Chrismated and follow a lifestyle that demonstrates faith that Christ is Lord and Savior. They become God's temple—in which holiness pervades to the degree they allow. No one can be dedicated to both God and idols (false gods). God is "jealous" (Ex 20:5) in that He demands our total allegiance for our own good—our salvation.

At the time Paul wrote this epistle, Corinth was a pagan city. The lives of the Corinthians revolved around idol worship. Those who became Christians were expected to make an absolute break with that type of life because worship belongs only to the Creator.

> **FOOD FOR THOUGHT:** (e). Does this verse apply in any way to the Christian life in our times? Are there pagans (idol worshippers) in our midst?

6:17-18. Therefore, "Come out from among them and be separate, says the Lord. Do not touch what is unclean, and I will receive you. I will be a Father to you, and you shall be My sons and daughters, says the Lord Almighty." Paul quotes the Old Testament (Isa 52:11), God's word to the Hebrews to be His people, different than non-Jews who were considered unclean according to the Law. He tells the early Christians they too must be set apart from prevalent pagan influence and activity. They are to become imitators of God, just as young children imitate their parents and thereby learn and grow.

> And do not wonder that a man may become an imitator of God...He who takes upon himself the burden of his neighbor; he who, in whatever way he may be superior, is ready to help another who is deficient; he who, by distributing to the needy from what he has received from God, becomes a god to those who receive these benefits: he is an imitator of God. MATHETES[13]

God expects us to do no less. We must separate ourselves from the unclean, the ungodly in our society, as far as our thoughts and conduct. Yet at the same time we are called upon to love even our enemies, to be good examples to all, and to welcome any sincere seeker to the love of the Gospel. This delicate balance is difficult, but *with God all things are possible* (Mt 19:26). Above all, we must allow nothing in our lives which has the possibility of coming between us and God and drawing us away from Him. If we put Him first in all we do, He will claim us as His children, entitled to dwell with Him forever.

CHAPTER SIX

Food For Thought Comments

6(a). What regular reminders are Orthodox Christians given of the need to commit and recommit their lives to Christ?

During the celebration of the Divine Liturgy we are prompted often to "...commend ourselves and one another and our whole lives to Christ our God." These are valuable reminders of the purpose for life. They also continually offer occasions to pray for those who may need a nudge in the right direction.

6(b). How can the gifts of the Spirit be misused?

Gifts of the Holy Spirit are given for the purpose of bringing a person, and through him, others, to union with God. Their proper use promotes unity within the Church. Those who use these gifts to bring glory or worldly gain to themselves misuse them and cause divisions. This was the case with the Corinthian Christians in their use of the gift of tongues (see text and this study of 1 Cor 12).

6(c). What are the signs of pride?

A prideful person has distinguishing characteristics.

> First, there is a loudness in the proud man's talk, a bitterness in his silent moods; when he is pleased, his laughter is loud and profuse; when he is serious, he is gloomy beyond reason. There is rancor in his replies to questions, glibness in his speech; his words break out unrestrained by any seriousness of heart. Of patience he knows nothing; charity is a stranger to him; he is bold in insulting others, cowardly in bearing their insults. He does not easily render obedience except where what is commanded fits with his own wishes. He is not to be appeased when one admonishes him; he is weak in curtailing his own wishes, very stubborn when asked to yield to those of others. He is always doing his best to establish his own opinions, but never ready to bow to those of anyone else. Finally, though he is quite incapable

> of giving good counsel, he is always more ready to trust his own judgment than that of the elders. CASSIAN[14]

6(d). How does the principle behind Jesus' words: *Seek first the Kingdom of God and His righteousness, and all things shall be added to you* (Mt 6:33) apply to our modern lives?

If we have truly committed our lives to Christ and believe that through Him we can live eternally with God, we will be guided in all that we do by Christ's teachings and His example. Every decision we make will be shaped not by what would be best in terms of success or gain in the world but rather by what He would expect of us. When this principle becomes ingrained in us, our life will have a healthy balance. It will not be easy, but the truly good things will be ours, in this life and the next.

> When you suffer anything for Christ's sake, do not merely bear it nobly, but also rejoice. When you fast, leap for joy as if enjoying luxury; if you are insulted, react as if praised; if you spend, feel as if gaining; if you bestow on the poor, count yourselves to receive: for he that does not give in this manner will not give readily...In every virtue, compute not only the severity of the toils but also the sweetness of the prize...and you will readily enter into the contest and will live the whole time in pleasure. For nothing is as apt to cause pleasure as a good conscience. CHRYSOSTOM[15]

6(e). Does verse 6:16 apply in any way to the Christian life in our times? Are there pagans (idol worshippers) in our midst?

The setting is different in our day, but Paul's advice still applies. We are given life to have the opportunity to find God and grow in union with Him. Thus we were created with a space in our hearts that aches until it is filled by His presence (Acts 17:26-27). If something other than God becomes the most important element in our lives, be it career, money, power, fame, a person, or even sports or other forms of recreation, it takes God's rightful place. It becomes to us a false god—an idol—and we become idol worshippers. Idol worshippers have nothing in common with those who worship God, nor do they ever find true peace because they misuse the gift of life. It is crucial that we place God on His throne in our hearts and lives so all other elements will take their proper place.

CHAPTER SEVEN

On Being Set Apart from the World

BACKGROUND: Chapter Six ended with a reminder that those who separate themselves from the ungodly will have fellowship with God, in a relationship of Father to sons and daughters. Now Paul issues a call to the next step, growth in holiness.

7:1. Therefore, having these promises, beloved, let us cleanse ourselves from all filthiness of the flesh and spirit, perfecting holiness in the fear of God. God's promises to those who separate themselves from the ungodly produce hope and joy. They also should awaken fear, however, because they remind us that those who do not will be heir to that which they have reserved for themselves—eternity separated from God's goodness. Therefore, it behooves us to continue our efforts to be Christ-like in all areas of our lives, *perfecting holiness (2 Pet 3:9-15).* This necessitates being different, set apart from the world, not as elitists but to walk with and to lead others to Christ and to prepare for life in His Kingdom.

> Not only did Christ fulfill the prophecies and plant the word of truth, but also in these happenings He gave us guidance regarding our lives, providing us with a rule of conduct for every need; teaching us by every means how to live worthily. CHRYSOSTOM[1]

> **FOOD FOR THOUGHT:** (a).What are the attributes of holiness?

During the Divine Liturgy, before the invitation to receive the Body and Blood of Christ, we hear the words: "The Holy Things for those who are Holy." We respond: "One is Holy, One is Lord, Jesus Christ..." The Eucharist which is about to be offered is itself holy and is for the holy. But the stark reality is that no one is truly holy except our Lord Jesus. How then do we dare to approach to receive Holy Communion? By the grace of God, through which we become *a holy nation, His own special people* (1 Pet 2:9). We dare to take part in that which is reserved for the holy because we are a part of the Body of Christ through Baptism. We remain a part of Him and progressively partake of His holiness, *if*, as we are able, we continually try to become in our lives what He has already made us by grace. As long as we continue in this struggle we show our assent, our faith. By this faith we open ourselves to that which is holy, as Mary conceived Christ in her womb through the Holy Spirit the very moment she assented to the will of God (Lk 1:38). Her assent, however, was not just verbal. She lived in obedience to that which God asked of her in all ways, as she had prior to being visited by Archangel Gabriel. Those who do not engage in this struggle shut grace out of their lives and make themselves unworthy of that which is holy. The disobedient either do not really believe, no matter what they profess with their mouth, or they *know not what they do* (Lk 23:34).

> We partake of Holy Communion *only* because we have been made holy by Christ and in Christ; and we partake of it in order to become holy, i.e., to fulfill the gift of holiness in our life. It is when one does not realize this that one "eats and drinks unworthily"—when, in other terms, one receives Communion thinking of one's self as "worthy" through one's own, and not Christ's holiness; or when one receives it without relating it to the whole of life as its judgment, but also as the power of its transformation, as forgiveness, but also as the inescapable entrance into the "narrow path" of effort and struggle.[2]

7:2. Open your hearts to us. We have wronged no one, we have corrupted no one, we have defrauded no one. Paul introduces the element of trust. He feels he has earned a place in their hearts because of his unwavering care and concern for them. This is an important point. If we earn the love and trust of those around us through interaction with them in the day-to-day activities of life, our efforts to share the truths of the Gospel with them will bear more fruit.

7:3. I do not say this to condemn; for I have said before that you are in our hearts, to die together and to live together. Paul's admonishments are not meant as judgment of the

Corinthians. His intent is not to dismiss them from his care but to redirect them, where necessary, as God redirected him, and to remain their advocate through all that life brings.

> **FOOD FOR THOUGHT:** (b). It would seem that to *die together* would be more difficult than to *live together*; yet the writings of the Fathers of the Church suggest that giving love and support in good times is more difficult and rare than during times of adversity. How can this be?

7:4. Great is my boldness of speech toward you, great is my boasting on your behalf. I am filled with comfort. I am exceedingly joyful in all our tribulation. The good news Paul has received regarding their spiritual progress brings him great comfort, even during times of tribulation. With the strength he receives from God, he speaks out boldly to encourage greater virtue and a closer walk with Christ.

7:5-7. For indeed, when we came to Macedonia, our flesh had no rest, but we were troubled on every side. Outside were conflicts, inside were fears. Nevertheless God, Who comforts the downcast, comforted us by the coming of Titus, and not only by his coming but also by the consolation with which he was comforted in you, when he told us of your earnest desire, your mourning, your zeal for me, so that I rejoiced even more. When Paul left Troas and went to Macedonia from where he writes (2 Cor 2:12-13), he was upset at not finding Titus waiting for him. He faced continual persecution for the work he was doing and was troubled by fears that it was not bearing fruit. Then, finally, Titus arrived! His arrival brought Paul comfort and joy, especially when Titus shared the encouraging news that the Christians of Corinth were responding to Paul's first epistle and the reprimands it brought with the spirit in which they were intended. They were repentant for the errors of their ways and were eager for Paul to return.

7:8-9. For even if I made you sorry with my letter, I do not regret it; though I did regret it. For I perceive that the same epistle made you sorry, though only for a while. Now I

rejoice, not that you were made sorry, but that your sorrow led to repentance. For you were made sorry in a godly manner, that you might suffer loss from us in nothing. A wise parent admonishes his errant children, bringing temporary pain, in order to teach them and keep them from danger. In like manner, a spiritual father chastens when necessary to prompt repentance and correction of ways, to prevent their straying from God.

> To soothe that he may hurt is the way of the Devil. To chastise that He may bring us to greater good is the way of the Lord. So when things are going easily amid plenty, beware. CHRYSOSTOM[3]

It had saddened Paul to write his stern letter, but if he had refrained from correcting them for fear of hurting their feelings or becoming unpopular with them, he would have been guilty of allowing them to drift away from God.

> **FOOD FOR THOUGHT:** (c). What responsibility do the faithful bear towards those who consider themselves Christians yet seem to be following a way of life which is contrary to that prescribed by the Gospel?

7:10. For godly sorrow produces repentance to salvation, not to be regretted; but the sorrow of the world produces death. Godly sorrow produces repentance upon realization that one has been wrong spiritually. We should not regret producing godly sorrow. The sorrow of the world, on the other hand, is worthless because it is superficial, concerned only with physical comfort and pleasure rather than spiritual growth.

> And what is worldly? If you are in sorrow for money, for reputation, for one who has departed, all these are worldly. They also work death. For he who sorrows for reputation's sake feels envy and is driven oftentimes to perish: such was the sorrow Cain felt, such Esau. By worldly sorrow he means that which is to the harm of those who sorrow. For only in respect to sins is sorrow a profitable thing. He who sorrows for loss of wealth does

not repair that damage; he who sorrows for one deceased does not raise the dead to life again; he who sorrows for a sickness, not only is not made well but even aggravates the disease. He who sorrows for sins, alone attains some advantage from his sorrow, for he makes his sins wane and disappear. In this case only is it potent and profitable; and worldly sorrow is even harmful. "And yet Cain," one can say, "sorrowed because he was not accepted with God." It was not for this, but because he saw his brother glorious in honor; for had he grieved because he was not in good standing with God, he would have tried to emulate and rejoice with his brother; but, as it was, he showed that his was a worldly sorrow. But not so David, nor Peter, nor any of the righteous. They were accepted because they grieved over their own sins or those of others. And yet what is more oppressive than sorrow? Still when it is after a godly sort, it is better than the joy in the world. CHRYSOSTOM[4]

FOOD FOR THOUGHT: (d). What is the *death* that is produced by the *sorrow of the world*?

7:11. For observe this very thing, that you sorrowed in a godly manner: What diligence it produced in you, what clearing of yourselves, what indignation, what fear, what vehement desire, what zeal, what vindication! In all things you proved yourselves to be clear in this matter. The godly sorrow aroused in the Corinthian Christians by Paul's admonitions caused them to realize the error of their ways and to set about to correct them.

FOOD FOR THOUGHT: (e). Is it possible to bring about *godly sorrow* in the modern world?

7:12. Therefore, although I wrote to you, I did not do it for the sake of him who had done the wrong, nor for the sake of him who suffered wrong, but that our care for you in the sight of God might appear to you. The immoral relationship between the man and his stepmother (1 Cor 5:1) posed spiritual danger to the entire community. As their teacher, Paul must answer to God for his efforts to restore conditions that will allow spiritual health and growth. God's directives to His people are not meant to restrict them unnecessarily nor to make their lives difficult. On the contrary, their purpose is to lead them to joys unending—in this life and the next.

> **FOOD FOR THOUGHT:** (f). What does Paul's concern that he do his best *in the sight of God* to guide the Corinthians say to all Christians, especially to those who are entrusted with the care of others, like clergy, parents and godparents?

7:13-15. Therefore we have been comforted in your comfort. And we rejoiced exceedingly more for the joy of Titus because his spirit has been refreshed by you all. For if in anything I have boasted to him about you, I am not ashamed. But as we spoke all things to you in truth, even so our boasting to Titus was found true. And his affections are greater for you as he remembers the obedience of you all, how with fear and trembling you received him. Paul is elated that they responded positively to his letter and to Titus as his emissary. Titus' love for the Corinthians has grown as a result of their response to him and the seriousness with which they received the guidance he brought from Paul.

> He who has faith in the Lord fears chastisement; and this fear prompts him to keep the commandments. The keeping of the commandments leads him to endure affliction; and the enduring of affliction produces hope in God. Such hope separates the intellect from all material attachment; and the person freed from such attachment possesses love for God. Whoever follows this sequence will be saved. PETER OF DAMASKOS[5]

7:16. Therefore, I rejoice that I have confidence in you in everything. Confident of their love for Christ because of their affirming actions, Paul rejoices as does any parent who sees that his charges are on the right track.

> Nothing so distinguishes a leader as much as paternal affection for those he leads. Begetting alone does not constitute a father, but begetting and loving....Moses,

for the sake of those he led, left great riches and treasures untold, *choosing to suffer affliction with the people of God* (Heb 11:25). CHRYSOSTOM[6]

CHAPTER SEVEN
Food For Thought Comments

7(a). What are the attributes of holiness?

Holiness is godliness (Lev 11:44).

> Holiness does not mean chastity alone but freedom from every kind of sin, for he that is pure is holy. One will become pure if he is free from fornication, covetousness, envy, pride, and vainglory...It is important to avoid vainglory in everything, but especially in almsgiving (since it is not almsgiving, but display and cruelty, if it is tainted with vainglory)...in fasting, and in prayer.
>
> CHRYSOSTOM[7]

> We all accept that there is special training for philosophers, for teachers, for athletes. Equally, for those who have chosen to major in holiness, there is a special training in the word. It involves, as does any serious training, almost every detail of life: walking, eating, resting, working, every part is disciplined and every part contributes to the goal of spiritual health and beauty.
>
> Mind you, this training (unlike some of the others) does not put people under emotional or physical strain and tension. It is not a matter of driving oneself to the limit so much as allowing the word to show us our weaknesses and moral flaws and then bringing us the Savior's own remedies, precisely gauged to meet every specific need.
>
> CLEMENT OF ALEXANDRIA[8]

7(b). It would seem that to *die together* would be more difficult that to *live together;* yet the writings of the Fathers of the Church suggest that giving love and support in good times is more difficult and rare than during times of adversity. How can this be?

There are many who envy the good fortune of others, so find it difficult to rejoice when they prosper or are honored, while sympathizing with their misfortunes is easy. Envy shows lack of true love.

> Nothing more destructive springs up in the souls of men than the passion of envy, which, while it does no harm to others, is the dominant and peculiar evil of the soul that harbors it. As rust consumes iron, so does envy wholly consume the soul it dwells in. More than this, as vipers are said to be born through devouring the maternal womb, so envy devours the soul that gives it birth.
>
> BASIL[9]

7(c). What responsibility do the faithful bear towards those who consider themselves Christians yet seem to be following a way of life which is contrary to that prescribed by the Gospel?

God guides His people through His teachings, which have been passed on through the ages. The faithful try to direct their lives accordingly. Because of God's gift of free will, however, each person has the right to accept or to reject His guidance. This presupposes that all have had an opportunity to learn the fullness of His word and the obedience and spiritual growth it requires. To that end, each Christian should try to share its truths with those whose paths cross theirs, allowing them to make informed decisions about their lives on earth and beyond the grave. There are times when those who call themselves Christians engage in behavior or activity that is not Christ-like. In dealing with such instances, it is first of all important to remember that it is not our place to pronounce judgment upon others—judgment belongs to God.

> Let us not be overcurious about the failings of others, but take account of our own; let us remember the goodness of others, while we bear in mind our faults, and thus we shall be well pleasing to God. CHRYSOSTOM[10]

With that warning, however, it remains that there are times when someone might benefit spiritually from a firm nudge in the right direction—a loving gesture on the part of the one who makes such an attempt. Because we have no right to judge the person, the behavior or action in question must be our focal point.

> For example: a brother has fallen into fornication. Do not disgrace him because of his fault; but don't laugh at it either. You will do no good to whoever hears you; rather it is more likely that you will do him harm, goading him further. But if you advise him as to what he should do, you will do him a great favor: if you teach him to use speech fittingly, and guide him so that he will abuse no one, you will teach him exceedingly well, and you will have brought him grace. If you speak with him about repentance, of the love of God, of giving to the poor, all these things will heal his soul. For all this he will be grateful to you. But if you laugh at him or speak hurtfully to him, you will provoke him instead. If you show any approval of his evil doing, you will undo him and destroy him. CHRYSOSTOM[11]

To try to correct someone is probably one of the most difficult things we can attempt. Such an endeavor should only be undertaken with extreme caution and with prayer for discernment. It is usually best to wait for the right moment and then to lovingly do or say that which is most likely to bring repentance and healing.

> Keep in touch with them. Encourage them not to abandon their belief in the Lord's mercy towards those who repent. Assure them that if they humbly and sincerely confess their sins and turn back to God, He will receive them and give them his strength and support to change their way of life. CYPRIAN[12]

Social pressure among peers can be a very powerful influence for good or evil. The purpose of Christian correction or guidance must always be to preserve, intact, the Church and her teachings, and to try to bring the person involved into fuller fellowship with it. This must be done very carefully because harm may be done if he is lost to the Kingdom.

> Those who let us do as we like are neither good teachers nor good friends.[13]

> There is no credit in spending all your affection on the cream of your pupils. Try rather to bring the more troublesome ones to order by using gentleness. Nobody

> can heal every wound with the same unguent; where there are acute spasms of pain, we have to apply soothing poultices. So in all circumstances be *wise as the serpent, though always harmless as the dove* [Mt 10:16].
>
> IGNATIUS OF ANTIOCH[14]

7(d). What is the *death* that is produced by the *sorrow of the world?*

The death produced by worldly sorrow is not the Christian death through which one passes from this life to the fullness of the Kingdom. Rather, it is the end of any hope and joy that comes from association with the things of God.

> As you become imitators of God you will see, as you walk the earth, that there is a God Who is operative in Heaven; you will begin to focus on His mysteries; and you will know love and admiration for those who incur persecution by their refusal to deny Him. Then too, you will see through the deceitfulness and error of this world once you have found what it is to live the true life of Heaven and have learned to despise the seeming death of the body and to dread only the real death which is reserved for those condemned to the fires of eternity—fires that will torment their victims forevermore. In the knowledge of those fires, your admiration will go out to all who endure a more transient flame for righteousness sake, and you will call them blessed. MATHETES[15]

For more on the "fires of eternity," see Food For Thought Comments 5 (d) and (e).

7(e). Is it possible to bring about *godly sorrow* in the modern world?

The modern world provides fertile ground for producing the godly sorrow which leads to repentance. As society in general strays further and further from God and the values His word teaches, the quality of life declines. Selfish concerns dominate and life seems cold, cruel and meaningless. In such a setting, some begin to realize something is amiss, and they search for direction. If at this point they are taught or reminded about God's truths, sorrow—godly sorrow—can build in their hearts for the sad state of mankind. This can produce the fruit of repentance and subsequent renewal in the joy of life God intended. We can be helpful in this process by trying in every circumstance to share with others, in a non-judgmental way, that which God expects of His people—while at the same time acting in a loving manner toward everyone. Often the best way to do this is to be a good example, so perhaps those looking on who have strayed will realize their own lives are not following the path leading to God and will repent.

> When Christ was establishing laws for His Disciples, what did He command of them? Certainly not that they should perform wonders, that men might behold them. No. He said: *Let your light shine before men, that they may see your good works, and glorify your Father Who is in Heaven*. To Peter likewise He did not say: *If you love me work miracles*, but *Feed My sheep* (Jn 21:17). And since on all occasions He singles him out from the rest, together with James and John, I ask why did He single them out? Because of their miracles? But all the Apostles cleansed the lepers, and raised the dead. To all alike He gave this power. Why then were these three preferred? Because of the virtue of their lives and the magnanimity of their souls. See then the need of a good life and the need of fruitful works? *You shall know them by their fruits* (Mt 7:16). CHRYSOSTOM[16]

7(f). What does Paul's concern that he do his best *in the sight of God* to guide the Corinthians say to all Christians, especially to those who are entrusted with the care of others, like clergy, parents and godparents?

All who have been entrusted with the spiritual care of others have a very serious responsibility to do all they can to teach those dependent upon them about the wonders of God and His promises and will answer to Him in this regard. Because everyone has free will, however, we will not be judged by the extent to which these efforts were successful but by the care and discipline we exercised to do our best (see this study for 1 Cor 3:12-15).

> The priest, even if he disciplines his own life in a fitting manner, yet does not scrupulously have due care for both your life and the lives of those around him, shall go with the wicked into everlasting fire; and so he oftentimes, while not failing in his own conduct, will perish because of yours, if he has not done all that belonged to him to do.
>
> CHRYSOSTOM[17]

Lay members of the Church also bear responsibility for the care and nurturing of the spiritual lives of others. As part of the Body of Christ we all belong to the *royal priesthood*, called to proclaim His praises to all who will listen (1 Pet 2:9).

CHAPTER EIGHT
That Which is Considered Almsgiving

BACKGROUND: At the close of Chapter Seven, Paul expressed joy that the faith of the Corinthian Christians has been strengthened. He now points to the generous almsgiving of the Christians in Macedonia, from where he writes, to encourage further growth in this area of the spiritual lives of the Corinthians through emulation.

8:1-2. Moreover, brethren, we make known to you the grace of God bestowed on the churches of Macedonia: that in a great trial of affliction the abundance of their joy and their deep poverty abounded in the riches of their liberality. The Christians in Macedonia had suffered great persecution and had lost most of their worldly possessions. Yet through the grace of God which comes to those who are obedient to Him in spite of tribulation, they did not become despondent. On the contrary, they were filled with the joy of the Lord. Their love for God manifested itself in a generous offering for the poor of the church in Jerusalem, the mother church. Notice that Paul said *the riches of their liberality*, not of their gifts. The amount involved may have been small in comparison to that given by others but was abundant considering their situation.

> Just as their great affliction gave birth to great joy, their great poverty gave rise to greatness in almsgiving...for bountifulness is determined not by the measure of what is given but by the mind of those who bestow it.
>
> CHRYSOSTOM[1]

8:3-4. For I bear witness that according to their ability, yes, and beyond their ability, they were freely willing, imploring us with much urgency that we would receive the gift and the fellowship of the ministering to the saints. They gave willingly from the little they had and pleaded with Paul to use them and what they offered for his ministry.

Paul mentions three reasons to praise the Macedonians: that they bear trials nobly; that they know how to pity; and that, though poor, they are generous in almsgiving.
CHRYSOSTOM[2]

8:5. And this they did, not as we had hoped, but first gave themselves to the Lord and then to us by the will of God. Their response was beyond what Paul had hoped for because it was fruit of their strong commitment to Christ. They eagerly followed Paul's guidance in this and other spiritual matters because they recognized him as the one through whom God worked for their spiritual enrichment.

8:6. So we urged Titus, that as he had begun, so he would also complete this grace in you as well. Paul had urged Titus to continue his ministry to the Corinthians by giving them further guidance in almsgiving—a very important part of the Christian life.

FOOD FOR THOUGHT: (a). Is all giving considered almsgiving? Does God acknowledge giving which comes from those who do not believe in Him or His Son as the Messiah but who give because they are kind or because they like the gratitude their giving brings?

8:7-8. But as you abound in everything—in faith, in speech, in knowledge, in all diligence, and in your love for us—see that you abound in this grace also. I speak not by commandment, but I am testing the sincerity of your love by the diligence of others. Paul is not demanding that they give, nor dictating the amount. Almsgiving is a reflection of love. True love reaches outward to others.

Whatever fruits of kindness you yield, you gather up for yourself; for the grace of good works and their reward is returned to the giver. Have you given something to a person in need? What you have given becomes yours, and is returned to you with an increase. And as the wheat that falls to the earth brings increase to the one who has thrown it there, so the bread that you give to the

> hungry will later bring you a great gain. Therefore, let the end of your earthly tilling be the beginning of your heavenly sowing. BASIL[3]

8:9. For you know the grace of our Lord Jesus Christ, that though He was rich, yet for your sakes He became poor, that you through His poverty might become rich. Jesus set the ultimate example of giving. He gave Himself completely, with love as the only motive. He became poor at His Incarnation when He willingly took on a form beneath His heavenly status in glory, power, and position (Phil 2:5-8) so He could unite man with God. Through Him man has access to the riches of Heaven:

> ...knowledge of godliness, cleansing away of sins, justification, sanctification, the countless good things which He bestows upon us and wants to bestow upon us.
> CHRYSOSTOM[4]

> **FOOD FOR THOUGHT:** (b). Must we rid ourselves of all earthly possessions in order to be part of the Kingdom of Heaven?

8:10-11. And in this I give my advice: It is to your advantage not only to be doing what you began and were desiring to do a year ago; but now you also must complete the doing of it; that as there was a readiness to desire it, so there also may be a completion out of what you have. In his first epistle Paul told the Corinthians to begin thinking of what they would give for the work of the Church (1 Cor 16:1-2). He now urges them to complete their collection, to act on their stated intentions.

Here Paul addresses an ever-present danger. Often, after hearing an inspiring sermon or reading a spiritually enlightening book, we are prompted to take a look at our spiritual life. We may vow to do better, to try harder or to give more but then forget those good intentions when we get back into the routine of daily living. It is important that we guard against this lack of spiritual discipline. God honors the intentions of our heart if we are prevented from fulfilling them by circumstances beyond our control but not if they die from neglect.

> For what they hear in instructions is indeed pleasing to many people, and they set about the beginning of good works: but soon being wearied by the afflictions that come to them, they abandon the good they have begun.
> GREGORY THE GREAT[5]

8:12. For if there is first a willing mind, it is accepted according to what one has and not according to what he does not have. God does not expect everyone to give in equal amounts but to give gladly, according to means.

> For what is much and what little God defines, not by the measure of what is given but by the extent of the substance of him that gives. CHRYSOSTOM[6]

8:13-14. For I do not mean that others should be eased and you burdened; but by an equality, that now at this time your abundance may supply their lack, that their abundance also may supply your lack—that there may be equality. The church in Jerusalem is rich spiritually but very poor in material effects. Paul is not asking that the Corinthians give to the point of poverty but from their abundance.

> You are flourishing in money; they in holiness of life and in boldness towards God. Give to them, therefore, of the money in which you abound but they have not; that you may receive of that boldness wherein they are rich and you are lacking. CHRYSOSTOM[7]

8:15. As it is written, "He who gathered much had nothing left over, and he who gathered little had no lack." Exodus 16 relates that when the Israelites were journeying through the wilderness, after Moses led them out of Egypt, they began to complain because they were hungry. So the Lord said to Moses: *I will rain bread from Heaven for you. And the people shall go out and gather a certain quota every day, that I may test them, whether they will walk in My law or not.* They were told to gather what they needed for their family: *one omer for each person.* No matter how much anyone gathered, they found they had neither a surplus nor a shortage—God's way of teaching them to be satisfied that their basic needs were met.

> ...and to persuade them never to desire to have more nor to grieve at having less. CHRYSOSTOM[8]

They were expected to work, gathering that which God had provided, to the extent each was able. He who was able to gather an abundance could not expect to have more for himself than anyone else. Likewise, he who worked diligently but was unable to fill his quota could be assured that he and his family would not go hungry.

> **FOOD FOR THOUGHT:** (c). What is the present day message of this verse? What is the difference between modern communistic principles and this Christian method of the sharing of resources? (d). Exodus 16:16-24 relates that God told the people to gather only what they needed daily, and to save (hoard) none till the following morning. When they disobeyed, the following morning what they had hoarded *bred worms and stank.* Yet God told them that on the sixth day they could gather a double portion so they would have enough for their needs on the Sabbath, a day of rest, when work was not allowed. On the Sabbath, that which they had saved from the day before *did not stink, nor were any worms in it.* Why? What are the present-day analogies of this incident?

8:16-19. But thanks be to God, Who puts the same earnest care for you into the heart of Titus. For he not only accepted the exhortation, but being more diligent, he went to you of his own accord. And we have sent with him the brother whose praise is in the Gospel throughout all the churches, and not only that but who was also chosen by the churches to travel with us with this gift, which is administered by us to the glory of the Lord Himself and to show your ready mind... Paul is grateful for the love and concern Titus exhibits for the Corinthians and for the zeal of his ministry to them. Though it is a long, hard journey, he has agreed to return to them in advance of Paul's visit to help them understand the merits of almsgiving as Paul requested (2 Cor 8:6) and to help them with the practical application—the collection of the offering. The brother mentioned, who would share responsibilities with Titus, was thought by Chrysostom to be Barnabus.

8:20-23. avoiding this: that anyone should blame us in this lavish gift which is administered by us—providing honorable things, not only in the sight of the Lord, but also in the sight of men. And we have sent with them our brother, whom we have often proved diligent in many things but now much more diligent because of the great confidence which we have in you. If anyone inquires about Titus, he is my partner and fellow worker concerning you. Or if our brethren are inquired about, they are messengers of the churches, the glory of Christ. Apparently Paul expects their offering to be substantial. He takes great care to insure that no one find fault with its collection or distribution. He is sending to collect it, three fellow workers whose reputations are above reproach. They will take this second epistle along with them. Paul assures the Corinthians that he will oversee the distribution of their offering so those who contribute will feel assured that the funds will not be misused.

> **FOOD FOR THOUGHT:** (e). The collection and utilization of funds is something with which every church community must be concerned. What can be learned from these verses? Is the spiritual value of our almsgiving negated if the money we give is misused?

8:24. Therefore show to them, and before the churches, the proof of your love and of our boasting on your behalf. Paul has praised the Corinthians for their spiritual growth. He has given them the example of the Christians in Macedonia who gave beyond their means because of their love for Christ and His work and has assured them that their money will not be misused. Now he urges them to fulfill their pledge for the church in Jerusalem as proof of their love and faith. Paul's words are very clear: our actions prove our faith.

> **FOOD FOR THOUGHT:** (f). Why is almsgiving considered proof of love and faith?

CHAPTER EIGHT

Food for Thought Comments

8(a). Is all giving considered almsgiving? Does God acknowledge giving which comes from those who do not believe in Him or His Son as the Messiah but who give because they are kind or because they like the gratitude and adulation their giving brings?

To give alms is to give willingly and joyfully from our resources with the knowledge that all good things have their source in God and, therefore, belong to Him in the first place. Those who understand this bask in the joy that such giving brings to others and consider that ample reward.

Only that giving which is motivated by belief in God and His Son as Savior is profitable toward the Kingdom of Heaven. Giving must be an outgrowth of, not instead of, a Christ-centered life. If we give without pointing to God through a life which demonstrates faith, we do only a temporary good. Real value comes from helping others in this life while directing attention to God, Who alone can satisfy our ultimate need: to be with Him.

To give in order to receive, either praise or returned favors, is to serve one's self, not others, so is not almsgiving. We must strive to have what we give known only to God. If we accomplish this we will be storing up treasures in Heaven (Mt 6:1-4, 19-20).

> It is almsgiving when it is done with willingness, when with bountifulness, when you deem yourself not to give but to receive, when done as if you were benefited, as if gaining and not losing...For he who shows mercy on another ought to feel joyful, not annoyed. For how is it not absurd, if while removing another's downheartedness, you yourself are downhearted?...if you are downhearted because you have delivered another from downheartedness, you furnish an example of extreme cruelty and inhumanity....And why are you downhearted at all, for fear your gold will diminish? If such are your

> thoughts, do not give at all: if you are not quite sure that it is multiplied for you in Heaven, do not give. You seek recompense here. Why? Let your alms be alms and not bartering. CHRYSOSTOM[9]

8(b). Must we rid ourselves of all earthly possessions in order to be part of the Kingdom of Heaven?

As love for God and communion with Him grow, desire for the superfluous things of this world decreases, fostering greater almsgiving. This is why many Saints gave up all their worldly possessions to serve God. It is not necessary, however, to be "poor" to be part of the Kingdom of Heaven, but rather "poor in spirit" (Mt 5:3).

> The Kingdom of Heaven shall be given to those whom humility of soul commends rather than the absence of riches....It cannot be doubted that this blessing of humility is more easily attained by the poor than the rich: for while meekness is the companion of those who live in poverty, pride is familiar to the rich. Yet in many among the rich, that spirit is found which uses its abundance not to increase its own inflated pride but in works of goodness and which holds as its greatest gain that which it has bestowed in relieving the misery of another's want. It is given to every kind and rank of men to share in this virtue because those who are unequal in means can be equal in good will; and it does not matter how dissimilar they are in earthly possessions, provided they are found equal in spiritual riches. Blessed therefore is that poverty which is not deluded by a longing for temporal things, which does not hunger to be made rich in the treasure of this world but desires to grow rich in heavenly things. LEO THE GREAT[10]

He who realizes that all he has belongs to God and that he actually owns nothing in this life is poor in spirit, no matter the extent of his earthly possessions. Such a person uses that which he has been entrusted with by God to do God's work, whenever and wherever possible.

> Don't despise possessions. And don't despise profits either. After all, possessions are "possessed" by us: they are our servants, not our masters. And profits are "profitable," or they should be.
>
> Wealth is at our disposal, an instrument which can be used well or foolishly. How it is used doesn't depend on the instrument but on the person who is using it. If we use it well, it is a valuable servant—a servant which can do good things for us and for those who depend on us. If we use it badly, it is an unhelpful servant—a servant which causes us and our friends endless harm. We shouldn't blame what is blameless. Wealth in itself is neither good nor evil.
>
> So where does the blame lie for all the evil done in the name of money and possessions? Not in the things themselves: they are harmlessly neutral. The evil is in the mind of man himself—man who by the free will and moral independence God has given him manages what he owns. Human desires express themselves through a man's possessions—desire to impress others, perhaps, or competitive instincts, which drive him always to rival his affluent neighbor. But those desires can also be noble ones, and express themselves in noble ways. Our money can feed the hungry and clothe the poor.
>
> CLEMENT OF ALEXANDRIA[11]

When speaking to the young man who pridefully declared that he had followed God's Commandments all of his life, Jesus said: *If you want to be perfect, go, sell what you have, and give to the poor, and you will have treasure in Heaven; and come, follow Me* (Mk 10:17-22). In response, the young man walked away, *for he had great possessions* and they were very important to him. The wisdom Christ offered this young man was that he had not followed the Commandments as closely as he thought. The first is: *You shall have no other gods before Me* (Ex 20:3). Our "god" is whatever we put first in our lives. This young man's earthly possessions had become his god—though he did not realize it.

> Riches did not prevent the young man from coming to receive Baptism, and it is quite wrong to say, as some do,

> that the Lord told him to dispose of his wealth so he could be baptized. CLIMACUS[12]

An alcoholic who tries to recover from his dependency knows that even one drink can put him in danger of losing control over his craving for more and more. Similarly, some people have a need to hoard earthly possessions. Unable to keep a healthy attitude toward them, their possessions control them, and all their energies are directed toward increasing their acquisitions. Jesus knew that this particular young man was unable to maintain a spiritually healthy attitude toward what he owned. Freeing himself from them entirely would help him put his focus on spiritual rather than worldly treasure and would help him conquer his pride because "he would learn to accept the charity of others."[13]

> Why do you tremble at the thought of poverty, and pursue wealth so ardently? So you won't need anything from anyone?...Don't you see that we are all in need of one another. The soldier of the artisan, the artisan of the merchant, the merchant of the farmer, the slave of the free man, the master of the slave, the poor man of the rich, the rich of the poor, he who does not work of him who gives alms?
>
> ...He who receives alms serves a very great need, a need greater than any. For if there were no poor, the greater part of our salvation would be overthrown in that we would not have a place to bestow our wealth. So that even the poor man who appears to be more useless than any is the most useful of all. CHRYSOSTOM[14]

8(c). What is the present day message of 2 Cor 8:15? What is the difference between modern communistic principles and this Christian method of the sharing of resources?

God provides for the needs of His people, as He did with the Israelites. He counsels us to work hard so that we will be in a position to provide for our own needs and those of others (Eph 4:28). He expects us to make wise use of the gifts of life, circumstances and ability He has given us, within the confines of obedience to the type of life He asks us to live, and to leave the rest to Him. All that we are able to accomplish in our lifetime we owe to His gifts. Those born into fortunate circumstances, with special abilities, be they intellectual, physical, or material, are what they are with no initial credit to themselves. What counts in God's eyes is what we do with that which we have been given. He who has been given more with which to work (time, talent, treasure) is expected not to hoard but to give of his excess to help those whose abilities and opportunities are fewer (Lk 12:48).

> Whether you will it or not, you will leave the gold behind but the glory that is born of good works you carry back to the Lord, where, standing before our common Judge all the people shall call you their nourisher and their benefactor and give you those other names that signify kindness and humanity. BASIL[15]

The Gospel's principles of providing for others differ from communistic principles in that they are not intended to be enforced by a worldly authority. Rather, they find their power in the willing hearts of those touched by Christ's teachings. They encourage rather than destroy individual initiative.

> Help the afflicted. Comfort those in sorrow. You who are strong, help the weak. You who are rich, help the poor. You who stand upright, help the fallen and the crushed. You who are joyful, comfort those in sadness. You who enjoy all good fortune, help those who have met with disaster. Give something to God in thanksgiving that you are of those who can give help, not of those who stand and wait for it; that you have no need to look to another's hands but that others must look to yours. Grow rich, not only in substance but also in piety; not only in gold but also in virtue; or rather, only in virtue. Be more honored than your neighbor by showing more compassion. Be as God to the unfortunate by imitating the mercy of God.
> GREGORY OF NAZIANZUS[16]

8(d). Exodus 16:16-24 relates that God told the people to gather only what they needed daily, and to save (hoard) none till the following morning. When they disobeyed, the following morning what they had hoarded *bred worms and stank*. Yet God told them that on the sixth day they could

gather a double portion so they would have enough for their needs on the Sabbath, a day of rest, when work was not allowed. On the Sabbath, that which they had saved from the day before *did not stink, nor were any worms in it.* Why? What are the present day analogies of this incident?

The message in being allowed to gather double on the sixth day in order to have enough for the seventh is that God understands our need to make reasonable provisions for ourselves if we obey His precepts along the way. When the Israelites disobeyed His instructions, the portion they hoarded became contaminated, rendering that which was given for their benefit potentially harmful to them. God did not create evil. When He finished His creation He pronounced every element in it "good" (Gen 1:31). Man's fall, eviction from Eden and the evils of the world they subsequently found themselves in were caused by misuse of that which was good. Modern examples of this abound:

God created the grape from which man learned to make wine. Jesus' first miracle involved turning water into wine for the enjoyment of the guests at the wedding in Cana (Jn 2). More importantly, it was a prefiguration of the wine which became His Blood at the Mystical Supper (Mt 26:27-28). Therefore, wine is used in the Sacrament of Eucharist, during which it becomes the Blood of Christ and is received by those who love Him, "for remission of sins and life everlasting." Yet some abuse the use of wine, and this abuse can lead to sin and destruction. The grape which God created is good, and wine made from the grape is used in the Church for the continuation of that which is good, but through improper use of them, man can bring about evil.

God instructed man to unite with woman to form a family and to multiply and fill the earth (Gen 1:27-28, 2:21-24). Within this framework, sexual intercourse is good—a wondrous gift from God to be enjoyed within marriage. Yet some use this gift in ways He has warned us not to—for our own well being. The shattered lives, abuses and diseases which often result are the consequences of misuse of one of His most powerful gifts.

Whether in regard to sexual behavior, lifestyles or spirituality, God's laws were given to set His people apart, to demonstrate that they are different from the rest of the world; to give them a way to show obedience through guidelines which, of their own free will, they must choose to obey or disobey; and to produce a better, healthier way of life on earth, with the fullness of God's Kingdom as the goal.

> You have tasted the fruit of disobedience. You have learned how bitter the food of that bitter counsellor. Taste now the food of obedience, which keeps evil away; and then you will learn that it is sweet and profitable to obey God. CYRIL OF ALEXANDRIA[17]

8(e). The collection and utilization of funds is something with which every church community must be concerned. What can be learned from these 2 Cor 8:20-23? Is the spiritual value of our almsgiving negated if the money we give is misused?

Those in authority must be sure that the methods and individuals involved in the collection and distribution of money are above reproach so those who are being asked to give will have no cause to doubt that their offering will be used for good purposes. If these basic criteria are satisfied, those who give should not allow doubts to hamper their giving. God honors the intentions of the giver, even if the funds are ultimately misused.

8(f). Why is almsgiving considered proof of love and faith?

Jesus said, *Where your treasure is, there your heart will be also* (Mt 6:21). It is easy to see what means most to a person by the allocation of his or her time, talent and treasure. Those who really love God give of their treasure so that His work will be done and His people cared for.

> Trials are of two kinds. Either affliction will test our souls as gold is tried in a furnace and make trial of us through patience, or the very prosperity of our lives will oftentimes, for many, be itself an occasion of trial and temptation. For it is equally difficult to keep the soul upright and undefeated in the midst of afflictions as to keep oneself from insolence and pride in prosperity.
> BASIL[18]

Let us think with shame of the great benefits we have already received and the great benefits we are yet to receive. If a poor man comes to us and begs, let us receive him with much good will: comforting him, encouraging him, so that we may be treated likewise, both by God and our fellowmen (Mt 7:12). CHRYSOSTOM[19]

CHAPTER NINE
To Encourage a Rich Harvest

BACKGROUND: Paul ended Chapter Eight by urging the Corinthians to give their offering for the Christians in Jerusalem, who were in desperate need, as a demonstration of their love for Christ. He goes on to share the blessings of almsgiving with them.

9:1-2. Now concerning the ministering to the saints, it is superfluous for me to write to you; for I know your willingness, about which I boast of you to the Macedonians, that Achaia was ready a year ago; and your zeal has stirred up the majority. Notice Paul's wisdom. In 2 Cor 8:1-5, he used the example of the generosity of the Christians in Macedonia, who gave willingly though they themselves were in great need, in order to encourage the Corinthians to imitate this good example. Here he confides that in order to encourage the generosity of the Macedonians, he had likewise boasted to them about the zeal of the Corinthian Christians.

9:3-5. Yet I have sent the brethren, lest our boasting of you should be in vain in this respect, that, as I said, you may be ready; lest if some Macedonians come with me and find you unprepared, we (not to mention you!) should be ashamed of this confident boasting. Therefore I thought it necessary to exhort the brethren to go to you ahead of time, and prepare your bountiful gift beforehand, which you had previously promised, that it may be ready as a matter of generosity and not as a grudging obligation. Paul is sending Titus and two other fellow-workers ahead to be sure the offering the Corinthians have promised will be ready. If Paul is accompanied by someone from the church in Macedonia when he arrives, he does not want his boasting about them to seem unfounded and thereby bring embarrassment to all concerned.

> **FOOD FOR THOUGHT:** (a). By what methods did Paul encourage spiritual growth in those he taught? Which of these is most effective?

9:6. But this I say: He who sows sparingly will also reap sparingly, and he who sows bountifully will also reap bountifully. To give so God's work may be done and His people cared for is to plant seeds of faith, hope, love, courage and joy. The more seeds we plant, the more of a harvest we can expect (Gal 6:7-9).

> Do you not know that we live in a foreign land, as though strangers and travelers? Do you not know that it is the lot of travelers to be ejected when they think not, expect not, which is also our lot. For this reason then, whatever we have acquired, we leave here. For the Lord does not allow us to take anything with us. If we have built houses, if we have bought fields, if any other such thing, not only does He not allow us to take them and depart, but does not even credit us with the price of them...
>
> The just, although having nothing, will both dwell here amidst all men's possessions as though they were his own; and also, when he has departed to Heaven, shall see those his eternal habitations. And he shall both here suffer no discomfort...and when he has been restored to his own country, shall receive the true riches. In order that we may gain both the things of this life and of that, let us use rightly the things we have. For so shall we be citizens of the heavens. CHRYSOSTOM[1]

9:7. So let each one give as he purposes in his heart, not grudgingly or of necessity; for God loves a cheerful giver. Christ gave the ultimate, His life, willingly. Though few are called upon to literally follow in His footsteps all the way to the Cross, those who call themselves Christians must strive to be like Him in all ways, including giving, so that His work may continue. Those who have means should give joyfully to help those who do not (read Deut 15:7-11).

> Make a little chest for the poor at home, near the place where you stand praying. As often as you pray, first deposit your alms, and then send up your prayer. As you would not wish to pray with unwashed hands, neither do so without alms...If you have this little coffer you have a defense against the Devil, you give wings to your prayer,

> you make your house holy, having meat for the King (Mt 25:34-36). CHRYSOSTOM[2]

9:8. And God is able to make all grace abound toward you, that you, always having all sufficiency in all things, have an abundance for every good work. As God provided seed to all living matter of His creation so that propagation is assured, He provides the means whereby His people are able to do that which He asks of them. If we plant a seed and nurture it, it will produce a harvest of its kind and a multiplicity of new seeds to continue the ever-expanding cycle. So too, if we manage to give of ourselves and our treasures without expecting any type of recognition or reward on earth, God will bless our efforts. Through His grace, all our *reasonable* needs will be met and we will have an abundance from which to help others. No one can outgive God.

> I am not leading you to entire poverty, but for the present I require you to cut off superfluities and to desire a "sufficiency" alone...That is superfluous which is more than we need. When we are able to live healthfully and respectably without a certain thing, then certainly that thing is superfluous.
>
> Thus let us think also in regard of clothing and of food and of a dwelling and of all our other wants, and in everything inquire what is necessary. For what is superfluous is also useless. When you have practiced living on what is sufficient, then if you have a mind to emulate that widow (Lk 21:2), we will lead you on to greater things than these. For you have not yet attained to the philosophy of that woman while you are anxious about what is sufficient. For she soared higher even than this; for what was to have been her support, that she cast in, all of it. CHRYSOSTOM[3]

FOOD FOR THOUGHT: (b). What spiritual wisdom can we glean from Chrysostom's words regarding superfluous "things"?

9:9. As it is written: "He has dispersed abroad, He has given to the poor; His righteousness remains forever." Quoting

Ps 112:9, Paul reflects that when we give as a consequence of love and faith, God remembers. In the measure we give, so we receive, in this life and the next because almsgiving is an indication of a purified heart and soul.

> The merciful man is not arrayed in a vest reaching to the feet, nor does he carry about bells nor wear a crown; but he is wrapped in the robe of loving kindness...holier than the sacred vestment and is anointed with oil, not composed of material elements but produced by the Spirit. He bears a crown of mercies, for it is said, *Who crowns you with lovingkindness and tender mercies* (Ps 103:4). Instead of wearing a plate bearing the Name of God, He is himself like God. CHRYSOSTOM[4]

> **FOOD FOR THOUGHT:** (c). Is there spiritual value in giving from ill-gotten gains? (Read 1 Sam 15:22-23).

9:10-14. Now may He who supplies seed to the sower and bread for food supply and multiply the seed you have sown and increase the fruits of your righteousness, while you are enriched in everything for all liberality, which causes thanksgiving through us to God. For the administration of this service not only supplies the needs of the saints but also is abounding through many thanksgivings to God, while through the proof of this ministry they glorify God for the obedience of your confession to the Gospel of Christ and for your liberal sharing with them and all men, and by their prayer for you, who long for you because of the exceeding grace of God in you. When those in need are ministered to by God's people, the harvest is great. Those who receive assistance are grateful that their suffering is relieved because of God's word to His people; the ministry of the teacher is shown to be effective; and the good example of those who give generously encourages love, fellowship, prayer and spiritual growth among those looking on. All this comes together through the grace of God. Nothing good can be accomplished without grace, but grace is actuated only when man cooperates with God's will.

> When you see a poor believer, think that you behold an altar...you honor the altar in the church because it receives Christ's Body; but he who is himself the Body of Christ, you treat with rudeness and neglect...When you see such a beggar you must not only refrain from insulting him, but even reverence him, and if you see another insulting him, prevent it, repel it...Do you want to see the altar built by God Himself?...The priest enters into the holy of holies. Into yet more awesome places you may enter when you offer this sacrifice, where none is present but *your Father Who sees in secret* (Mt 6:4)...What is the smoke, what the sweet savor of this altar? Praise and thanksgiving. And how far does it ascend? As far as unto Heaven? By no means—it passes beyond Heaven itself—and the Heaven of Heaven, and arrives at the throne of the King. For He says *your* prayers *and your alms have come up before God* (Acts 10:4). CHRYSOSTOM[5]

9:15. Thanks be to God for His indescribable gift! The gift which words cannot describe is God's divine plan for the salvation of mankind through His Son. An important part of this plan is the method by which the physical and spiritual needs of all are met through love and sharing. He who lives the Christ-like life that is called for under this plan has access to God's grace and is blessed with all good things: the glorious riches of the Kingdom which begin in this life and extend into eternity.

> God's riches are strong faith, firm hope, ardent love and good works.[6]

CHAPTER NINE
Food for Thought Comments

9(a). By what methods did Paul encourage spiritual growth in those he taught? Which of these methods is most effective?

Paul fostered spiritual growth in those he taught by encouraging them (2 Cor 7:4,7,11,14-16; 8:7), by pointing to the good examples of others (2 Cor 8:1-5), by reminding them of Christ's example (2 Cor 8:9) and His teachings, and by praying for them (2 Cor 13:9).

Christ's teachings engender knowledge of and thus love for Him. For the maturing Christian, they are, therefore, powerful tools towards spiritual growth. For someone just beginning to learn about Christ, however, encouragement and good examples are probably most effective. A hardened heart is not receptive to the seeds of faith. Man learns to love only after he receives love. The sower who first softens the heart encourages a greater harvest. Prayer is a powerful tool in any circumstance.

9(b). What spiritual wisdom can we glean from Chrysostom's words regarding superfluous "things"?

They remind us of the principle of keeping our desires in bounds, restrained by the needs of others. To be concerned only with ourselves causes withdrawal and isolation and separates us from the rest of the Body of Christ. If we realize that we do not need the biggest, the best, or the most of everything, we will always have a surplus from which to help others and to give to God's work. If we do not grow in this direction, we will never find the occasion to give because there is always something more to gather for ourselves.

> Possessions are external things, but our desires are within us. It is quite useless to try to reform the external objects if we have not first resolved the internal motivation. We may give all our money away, but what use is that if the longing for it still burns inside us? Poor people can covet. Poor people can envy. And poor people can misuse the little money they have. Getting rid of our

> material possessions will do nothing, in itself, to create in us a right attitude towards them.
>
> The real test always lies in our attitudes. We can enjoy our possessions, seeing them as God's generous gifts, and using them as much for others as for ourselves. We can possess them without allowing them to possess us.
>
> Only then can we be quite sure that if, in God's will, we are ever deprived of them, we may accept their loss as contentedly as we did their superabundance.
>
> CLEMENT OF ALEXANDRIA[7]

9(c). Is there spiritual value in giving from ill-gotten gains? (Read 1 Sam 15:22.)

To relieve another's distress from ill-gotten gains is to give a mixed message—the end does not justify the means.

> Nothing equals the merit of almsgiving. Great is the power of this action when it flows from untarnished sources, but when it comes from sources that are defiled, it is as if a fountain were to send forth mud. When alms are given from our just gains, it is as if they flowed forth from a pure and limpid stream, one flowing from paradise, pleasant to the eye, pleasant to the touch, something cool and light given in the noonday heat. Such are alms. Beside this fountain grow, not poplars nor pines nor cypresses but trees more rare and precious: the love of God, the praise of men, glory before God, the good will of all, the wiping away of sins, great confidence in God, and small esteem for riches. CHRYSOSTOM[8]

We cannot bribe God or appease Him with token gifts. Almsgiving is a part of the Christ-like life, not a substitute for it.

CHAPTER TEN

The Struggle Against Ungodly Forces

BACKGROUND: In writing this epistle, one of Paul's primary objectives is to establish his credentials as an Apostle, in answer to his detractors who question his authority to teach the Gospel. They accuse him of being weak and ineffective when among the Corinthians but bold in his letters to them from the safety of distance.

10:1. Now I, Paul, myself am pleading with you by the meekness and gentleness of Christ—who in presence am lowly among you, but being absent am bold toward you. With irony, Paul refers to the misconception of his personality held by his enemies. He is generally *meek and gentle*, in imitation of Christ, which his enemies perceive as weakness; but, also like Christ, he is capable of great boldness and righteous anger when confronted with false teachings or sinful conduct (Mk 11:15-17). The Hebrew word for *meek* actually means "capable of being molded." The original Greek word for *gentleness* means, more precisely, "forbearance." To be meek and gentle in the context of Scripture means to be willing to let God mold us in His image, according to His will, and to have self-control and patience under adverse conditions. Those who succeed in this are not weak, but strong.

> **FOOD FOR THOUGHT:** (a). Does being meek and gentle like Christ necessitate allowing oneself to be manipulated or to be intimidated into watering down expressions of faith so as not to offend? What is the proper Christian attitude toward non-believers?

10:2-3. But I beg you that when I am present I may not be bold with that confidence by which I intend to be bold against some who think of us as if we walked according to the flesh. For though we walk in the flesh, we do not war according to the flesh. True Christians are like everyone else in that they live in the world and are subject to the consequences of fallen human nature. But those who love God are also spiritual beings. They continually engage in spiritual warfare against those forces that want to prevent them from fulfilling their potential of union with God. Paul hopes he will not have to contend spiritually with the disobedient in the church in Corinth when he arrives.

> With all our strength let us hold fast to Christ, for there are always those who struggle to deprive our soul of His presence; and let us take care lest Jesus withdraws because of the evil thoughts that crowd our soul (Jn 5:13). Yet we will not manage to hold Him without great effort on the soul's part. Let us study His life in the flesh, so that in our own life we may be humble. Let us absorb His sufferings, so that by emulating Him we may endure our afflictions patiently. Let us savor His ineffable incarnation and His work of salvation on our behalf, so that from the sweet taste in our soul we may know that the Lord is bountiful (Ps 34:8). Also, and above all, let us unhesitatingly trust in Him and in what He says; and let us daily wait on His providence toward us. And whatever form it takes, let us accept it gratefully, gladly and eagerly, so that we may learn to look only to God, Who governs all things in accordance with the divine principles of His wisdom. If we do all these things, we are not far from God. PHILOTHEOS OF SINAI[1]

10:4. For the weapons of our warfare are not carnal but mighty in God for pulling down strongholds... Satan uses individuals, institutions and philosophies to help him achieve his goal of leading people away from God. In doing so, he creates strongholds which are difficult to stand against. But God has provided those who love Him with truth, righteousness, peace, and the Cross of Christ, as protection against Satan's attacks.

The disciplines of prayer (which includes fasting), watchfulness and perseverance strengthen us from within. When we use these spiritual weapons to help us live a Christ-like life, we deliver a mighty blow to the Devil's ambitions, against which he cannot stand (see Eph 6:10-18).

A modern example of the battle the true Christian engages in is provided by the success Satan has achieved in so distorting society's moral sense that a large segment of the world's population has no understanding or acceptance of the absolute truths revealed to man by God. His universal standard of right and wrong is not widely recognized—everything is relative. Sin is rationalized away. The sinner is absolved from personal responsibility, always able to find someone or something to blame. Real heroes are few, and the more outrageously and irresponsibly one behaves, the more attention he attracts. The general public has a startling fascination with athletes and movie idols, who seem to set society's standards. The only way a Christian can stay on the road to God in this environment is to fortify himself with scriptural truths and spiritual disciplines.

> The baptized Christian must struggle with his whole free will so that in true cooperation with God he will be able to reach a condition of unity with God. This journey is called the Christian life.[2]

Carnal weapons are those things in life that Satan tries to make seem of most importance:

> Wealth, glory, power, fluency, cleverness, circumventions, flatteries, hypocrisies, whatsoever else is similar to these. CHRYSOSTOM[3]

Many individuals use most of the precious time from their lives trying solely to amass these carnal weapons, though they are useless in the only battle that really matters—the spiritual battle to stay on the road to God. Sometimes individuals (clergy and laity) become a part of the Church for the wrong reasons: political and social connections membership may offer or the worldly power or prestige a position in the Church may bring. This is contrary to the message of the Gospel but should surprise no one because it has always been thus. Of the twelve Apostles Jesus chose, one was motivated primarily by financial considerations (Jn 12:6).

FOOD FOR THOUGHT: (b). With His foreknowledge, Jesus knew Judas would betray Him. Yet He chose him as an Apostle. Why? (c). Should offenders of the Gospel be routed from the Church?

10:5. casting down arguments and every high thing that exalts itself against the knowledge of God, bringing every thought into captivity to the obedience of Christ... Through the power of the spiritual weapons God gives His people, every intellectual argument, social force or act of the will against Him can be shattered and brought under subjection to Christ. With these weapons at his command, Paul brought many to the Kingdom and subdued many who were its enemies (read Acts 19:11-12, 17-20).

10:6. and being ready to punish all disobedience when your obedience is fulfilled. Paul has delayed his return to Corinth to give the faithful a chance to show their love by separating themselves from the false apostles who cause disruption in the Church. Upon his return, he intends to deal with the disobedient to restore harmony.

10:7. Do you look at things according to the outward appearance? If anyone is convinced in himself that he is Christ's, let him again consider this in himself, that just as he is Christ's, even so we are Christ's. True Christians develop spiritual gifts as fruit of their struggle to grow in holiness. One of these gifts is the ability to discern right from wrong, good from bad. Those who have this gift are not deceived by outward appearances, so would not be fooled by Paul's detractors who speak against him. They would recognize him as a man of God (Heb 5:12-14,1 Cor 2:14).

FOOD FOR THOUGHT: (d). How does one acquire the gift of discernment? Of what assistance is this gift in the Christian life?

10:8-11. For even if I should boast somewhat more about our authority, which the Lord gave us for edification and not

for your destruction, I shall not be ashamed—lest I seem to terrify you by letters. "For his letters," they say, "are weighty and powerful, but his bodily presence is weak, and his speech contemptible." Let such a person consider this, that what we are in word by letters when we are absent, such we will also be in deed when we are present. Paul refrains from expounding upon the power and authority God has given him because he does not want to give credence to his detractors' claims that he tries to intimidate them with his letters. Those who accuse him of being weak and ineffective in person will find that he is as bold and powerful as his letters when necessary.

10:12-13. For we dare not class ourselves or compare ourselves with those who commend themselves. But they, measuring themselves by themselves, and comparing themselves among themselves, are not wise. But we will not boast beyond limit, but will keep to the limits God has apportioned us, to reach even to you. Paul was chosen by God to bring His word to certain areas, one of which is Corinth (Acts 18:1-11). He, therefore, compares himself with the Apostles, chosen by God for the specific task of bringing Christ's Gospel to the world (Mt 28:19)—not with those who create their own agenda, with their own rules, and then boast about themselves without basis and authority. When Paul stresses his power and authority, he does so not in a boastful, dictatorial manner, but to put himself in a position from which he can carry out his mission. To shrink from that position in the name of modesty or humility would be to make himself impotent, unable to fulfill his responsibilities.

This verse also speaks well to the variable morality of our society. Many extol the virtue of "values," but unless those values are grounded in God's truths, they mean something different to each person.

10:14-16. For we are not extending ourselves beyond our sphere (thus not reaching you), for it was to you that we came with the Gospel of Christ; not boasting of things beyond measure, that is, in other men's labors, but having hope, that as your faith is increased, we shall be greatly enlarged by you in our sphere, to preach the Gospel in the

regions beyond you, and not to boast in another man's sphere of accomplishment. Paul hopes his efforts in Corinth will bear fruit so that God will expand his mission to teach into other areas to which the Gospel has not yet been brought.

10:17. But "He who glories, let him glory in the Lord." Those who try to do the work of the Lord must not boast about what "they" have done, only what the Lord has done—sometimes through them.

> **FOOD FOR THOUGHT:** (e). Is it possible for God to work through modern man as He did through Paul?

10:18. For not he who commends himself is approved, but whom the Lord commends. God alone is Judge, through His Son. He will determine whose life showed faith through love and obedience to His truth, and whose did not. We are judges of ourselves to the extent that the degree of harshness with which we judge others will be the standard that God uses to judge us (Mt 7:1-2). What we say or think about ourselves is not what matters, but what God knows about us.

> **FOOD FOR THOUGHT:** (f). There are those who believe that each person should seek "his own" truth. What does this verse say to them?

CHAPTER TEN
Food For Thoughts Comments

10(a). Does being meek and gentle like Christ necessitate allowing oneself to be manipulated or intimidated into watering down expressions of one's faith so as not to offend? What is the proper Christian attitude toward non-believers?

To be meek and gentle like Christ requires that we not return evil for evil, no matter how reviled or provoked. However, we need not and should not be without strength of conviction. The Christian model is to pray for guidance, to try continually to grow in grace and in knowledge and to be bold in following through with what God expects of us.

> What should we do about those around us who are not believers? Certainly we should pray for them, not just occasionally or as a matter of routine but all the time, in the hope that they may have a change of heart and so find their way to God.
>
> But we should also give them every opportunity to learn the truth of Christ from us, not so much, perhaps, by preaching it to them in so many words, but by the way we behave toward them. Our attitude should reflect the attitude of Christ.
>
> So when they are hostile, meet them with gentleness. When they make angry accusations, respond with calm words. When they abuse you, pray for them.
>
> At the same time, don't compromise your beliefs or water them down to make them acceptable. It is possible to stand firm against violence and error while remaining perfectly calm and gentle. Don't be trapped into playing their game.
>
> Show them that we regard them as our brothers, children of the same Creator and simply want them to become also our brothers in Christ, sons of the same Father. Our

> attitude should be that of the Lord. If we imitate Him, we won't go wrong. IGNATIUS OF ANTIOCH[4]

10(b). With His foreknowledge, Jesus knew that Judas would betray Him. Yet He chose Judas as an Apostle. Why?

With the gift of free will with which man has been endowed from the beginning, each of us either tries to fulfill the purpose for which we were given life (to seek God and live in a way that will lead to union with Him—Acts 17:26-27); or he rejects or ignores God (there is no middle ground—Mt 12:30, Rev 3:16). God knows the outcome of our life, not because He wills the results, but because He is omniscient and has foreknowledge. He allows each of us to live our life (to act out what He foreknows) so that on Judgment Day we will all realize that we had a chance for eternal blessedness, and that His judgment is fair. Jesus chose Judas as an Apostle to illustrate this truth, though He knew the consequences for Himself.

As the parable of the *wheat* and the *tares* illustrates (Mt 13:24-30), the word of God is brought to everyone so they can hear it and desire the Kingdom of Heaven. Some choose instead a kingdom on earth, as did Judas. They are the "tares" (weeds, useless or harmful growth): those who allow the *enemy* to sow lies in their hearts. Wherever there is "wheat" (those who attempt to grow in holiness), Satan works hard to uproot it (Rev 12:17). God allows this because He chooses to allow the consequences of the gift of free will to take their course in each person's life in order that the gift be complete, and because many lessons are taught in this way.

> Do you think, Brothers, that the tares do not reach to high seats? Do you think they are all down among you, and none above? That we may not be such!...But I tell you, in the high seats there are good wheat and there are tares; as among the people there are good wheat and there are tares. Let the good be patient with the wicked; let those who do evil change their ways and become as the good. Let us all, if possible, come unto God. May we all, through His mercy, escape the wickedness of this world. Let us seek good days, for we are in the midst of

> days that are evil: but in these wicked days let us not blaspheme, that we may reach unto the good days.
> AUGUSTINE[5]

10(c). Should offenders of the Gospel be routed from the Church?

If it seems to us that someone in the Church is there for the wrong reasons, we must first remember that not everything is necessarily what it appears to be:

> We have to deal with an adversary who is a great liar...Yet we can rejoice that we have a Judge Whom our accuser cannot deceive. Had we a man as a judge, our enemy could invent for him as he willed; for there is no one more clever at inventing than the Devil. Even now it is he who invents all the false accusations made against the saints. Since his accusations avail nothing with God, he scatters them among men....he knows the evil he can work with them, unless the vigilance of faith resists him. And it is for this he circulates evil about the good: that the weak may then think they are not any good and so let themselves be carried away by their own evil desires and become corrupted, saying to themselves: Who is there that keeps a commandment of God? Or who observes chastity? And when a man believes that no one does, he himself becomes this "no one." It is in this way that the Devil works. AUGUSTINE[6]

Secondly, we must keep in mind that the Church is the best place for the spiritually unawakened or wavering to be—where perhaps the Holy Spirit can soften their hearts and bring about repentance. Whenever possible, actions and behavior should be evaluated against the precepts of Scripture and dealt with lovingly but firmly (see Chapter Seven, Food for Thought Comment (c)), but we should not judge the person—God is the Judge and only He can do that (see 1 Cor 4:3-5).

> We are anxious that, if it were possible, nothing that was evil should remain among the good. But it was said to us: *Let both grow until the harvest*. Why? Because you are prone to error.[7]

> Hear what He says: *Let both grow together until the harvest, and at the time of harvest I will say to the reapers, first gather the tares and bind them in bundles to burn them: but gather the wheat into my barn.* Why hasten then, zealous servants, He says? Do you see that the tares stand in the midst of the good growth, and you wish to uproot the bad? Remain quiet, it is not yet the time of harvest. Let it come, and let it reveal to you the true wheat. Why need you be angry? Why are you impatient that the bad should not be mixed with the good? They may be among you in the field, but in My barn they shall not be with you. AUGUSTINE[8]

10(d). How does one acquire the gift of discernment? Of what assistance is this gift in the Christian life?

God gives His spiritual gifts to those who indicate, by word and by deed, that they want them, so if we seek wisdom, we should ask for it (Jas 1:5). At the same time, we should study Scripture for the guidance it contains, as the *fair-minded* Jews did when confronted with Paul's teaching that Jesus was the Messiah Whom they had been taught to await (Acts 17:11). The other important tool to which we have access is the writings of the Fathers of the Church, which preserve the original understanding of God's word to His people. Just as practice makes perfect with any skill, it is important to apply all acquired spiritual knowledge and understanding to the problems and circumstances of life day by day—for we continue to learn and grow when we actually try to live the Christian life.

> For him who possesses it, discrimination [discernment] is a light illuminating the right moment, the proposed action, the form it takes, strength, knowledge, maturity, capacity, weakness, resolution, aptitude, degree of contrition, inner state, ignorance, physical strength and temperament, health and misery, behavior, position, occupation, upbringing, faith, disposition, purpose, way of life, degree of fearlessness, skill, natural intelligence, diligence, vigilance, sluggishness, and so on...It reveals the nature of things, their use, quantity and variety, as well as the divine purpose and meaning in each word or passage of Holy Scripture...and the significance of the interpretation given by the Fathers.[9]

> Discrimination is born of humility. On its possessor it confers spiritual insight, as both Moses and St. John Climacus[10] say: such a man foresees the hidden designs of the enemy and foils them before they are put into operation...Discrimination is characterized by an unerring recognition of what is good and what is not, and the knowledge of the will of God in all that one does.[11]
>
> He who lacks discrimination cannot achieve anything; while the person who possesses it is a guide to the blind and a light to those in darkness (Rom 2:19). We should refer everything to such a person and accept whatever he says, even if because of our inexperience we do not see its import as well as we would like. Indeed, he who has discrimination is to be recognized in particular from the fact that he is able to communicate the sense of what he says even to those who do not want to know it.
>
> PETER OF DAMASKOS[12]
>
> Among beginners, discernment is real self-knowledge; among those midway along the road to perfection, it is a spiritual capacity to distinguish unfailingly between what is truly good and what in nature is opposed to the good; among the perfect, it is a knowledge resulting from divine illumination, which with its lamp can light up what is dark in others. To put the matter generally, discernment is—and is recognized to be—a solid understanding of the will of God in all times, in all places, in all things; and it is found only among those who are pure in heart, in body and in speech.
>
> CLIMACUS[13]

10(e). Is it possible for God to work through modern man as He did through Paul?

In every age, God has worked through those who love Him. Abraham, Isaac, Jacob, Moses, Noah, Job, Daniel, the Holy Prophets, the Apostles, Martyrs, saints (ancient and modern, known and unknown) and ordinary people of every description have been instruments of His will. He can and will work through each of us if we ask Him to, allow Him to, and try at the same time to grow in obedience to His word. This is why, although the patristic age is generally considered to include those important Christian writers from the end of the first to the end of the eighth centuries A.D., it never really ends. Each age has the potential to produce a "Father" of the Church.

10(f). There are those who believe each person should "seek his own truth." What does 2 Corinthians 10:18 say to them?

There is only one eternal Truth: that which emanates from God. Self-created truths are delusional. They have no real power, except to confuse, distract and lead the misguided away from the unalterable, unchanging divine word. In so doing they help the Devil, the deceiver of the world (Rev 12:9), accomplish his goal of depriving as many as he can of the joys of the Kingdom, which, for the true believer, begin in this life. A seeker who learns to look inwardly for the solutions to life's problems will find that which has been absorbed into his being during his lifetime—but what he finds within may be true or it may be false. That which is not based on God can lead him to self-worship: idolization of himself via his own thoughts.

Christianity calls us to look to our Creator for the answers to the questions of life. We cannot know truth on our own, only in communion with God. If those who love God plant His words in the hearts and minds of those they can influence, they will be giving them access to His Truth, His values, His light, His power. When seeking Truth, it is logical to look to those precepts preserved, protected and taught by the historic, early Church before heresies divided the Body of Christ. This is the treasure Orthodoxy offers.

CHAPTER ELEVEN
Safeguarding the Inheritance

BACKGROUND: One of the dangers to the Christians in Corinth, who are still infants spiritually, is that they will be led astray by the teachings of false apostles. Paul, therefore, continues his efforts to strengthen his relationship with them. He hopes to remain a positive influence in their lives.

11:1. Oh, that you would bear with me in a little folly—and indeed you do bear with me. In the awkward position of having to defend his authority as an Apostle of Christ, Paul finds it distasteful to seem to be boasting about himself.

11:2. For I am jealous for you with godly jealousy. For I have betrothed you to one husband, that I may present you as a chaste virgin to Christ. Exodus 20:5 relates that God is *jealous*. But He covets what is best for the object of His affections rather than for Himself. He wants each of us in His Kingdom—not in Satan's. Paul feels the same type of jealousy toward the Corinthian Christians. Following the Old Testament pattern which refers to Israel as the bride of God (Is 54:5), Paul refers to the Church as the Bride of Christ. He has promised the church in Corinth to Christ and intends to present her pure and undefiled by false teachings.

11:3. But I fear, lest somehow, as the serpent deceived Eve by his craftiness, so your minds may be corrupted from the simplicity that is in Christ. Satan persuaded Eve to follow his lead rather than God's instructions. The false apostles are trying to persuade the Corinthians that what they teach is superior to the Gospel of Jesus Christ. Paul hopes to prevent a replay of the ancient tragedy which has occurred again and again throughout the ages. Each time someone is led away from the simple truth of salvation through Christ, the Devil rejoices.

> What therefore must we do? We must wholly deny him all belief; stop up our ears against him, and regard this seducer with hate. And the more he promises the more

> must we avoid him. This he did with Eve. For when he had filled her with false promises, it was then he utterly ruined her and brought unending misery upon her. He is an unpitying enemy, and he has set himself implacably to war against us. We do not seek our own salvation as eagerly as he seeks our ruin. Let us turn away from him, and not in word only but in deed. And let us do none of the things that give him pleasure. In this way all we do shall be pleasing to God. CHRYSOSTOM[1]

11:4-5. For if he who comes preaches another Jesus whom we have not preached, or if you receive a different spirit which you have not received, or a different Gospel which you have not accepted, you may well put up with it. For I consider that I am not at all inferior to the most eminent apostles. If someone were to give them a better understanding of Jesus and His Gospel than that which they received from Paul, they would do well to listen. But he taught them the fullness of the Gospel—no less than they would have received from Peter, James or John, who were considered the most eminent Apostles. Note that when Paul's authority to teach is questioned, he numbers himself with the chief Apostles so that his ministry retains the power it must and does have from God.

11:6. Even though I am untrained in speech, yet I am not in knowledge. But we have been thoroughly made manifest among you in all things. Paul was not a dazzling orator and did not pretend to be (1 Cor 2:1), but he was highly qualified to teach the Gospel. It had been revealed to him by Christ Himself (Gal 1:12), and the Corinthians had seen ample evidence of Christ working through him to recognize the legitimacy of his ministry.

11:7-9. Did I commit sin in abasing myself that you might be exalted, because I preached the Gospel of God to you free of charge? I robbed other churches, taking wages from them to minister to you. And when I was present with you, and in need, I was a burden to no one, for what was lacking to me the brethren who came from Macedonia supplied. And in everything I kept myself from being burdensome to you, and so I will keep myself. Though he had the right as an Apostle to be paid for the work he did (1 Cor 9:1-14), he refused any compensation from the Corinthian church. He lived simply, so his trade of tentmaking (Acts 18:3) provided for his meager needs. The Christians in Macedonia supplied what he lacked, a fact he refers to as robbery because the Macedonians supported him while he ministered to the Corinthians. His practice of not accepting remuneration from those he was ministering to at the time allowed him freedom to correct and chasten his flock when necessary.

11:10-12. As the truth of Christ is in me, no one shall stop me from this boasting in the regions of Achaia. Why? Because I do not love you? God knows! But what I do, I will also continue to do, that I may cut off the opportunity from those who desire an opportunity to be regarded just as we are in the things of which they boast. Paul plans to continue his style of ministry to give no one reason to doubt his motives and to thwart the pseudo-apostles who try to use the Corinthians for financial gain. He preaches and teaches to bring people to Christ, not for worldly advantage.

11:13-15. For such are false apostles, deceitful workers, transforming themselves into apostles of Christ. And no wonder! For Satan himself transforms himself into an angel of light. Therefore it is no great thing if his ministers also transform themselves into ministers of righteousness, whose end will be according to their works. Those who continuously try to demean Paul's authority call themselves apostles. They expect to be paid for their work and claim that fact as a sign of the validity of their ministry. According to their rationale, Paul accepted no compensation because even he did not think his ministry was of value. He writes that these deceivers pretend outwardly to be virtuous in order to mislead, winning followers and then leading them astray.

Satan traditionally works in this manner. He does not appear to his victims in horns and a tail as cartoonists depict him but transforms himself into something that appears righteous in order to gain souls through trickery. His ministers do likewise. Therefore, we must always be on guard.

> Deceitful workers pull up what has been planted. They wear the mask of truth because they are well aware that otherwise they would not be well received. CHRYSOSTOM[2]

FOOD FOR THOUGHT: (a). Why does God allow Satan and his workers to practice such deceit?

11:16-21. I say again, let no one think me a fool. If otherwise, at least receive me as a fool, that I also may boast a little. What I speak, I speak not according to the Lord, but as it were, foolishly, in this confidence of boasting. Seeing that many boast according to the flesh, I also will boast. For you put up with fools gladly, since you yourselves are wise! For you put up with it if one brings you into bondage, if one devours you, if one takes from you, if one exalts himself, if one strikes you on the face. To our shame, I say that we were too weak for that! But in whatever anyone is bold—I speak foolishly—I am bold also. The false apostles Paul alludes to at this point are Judaizers. They claim to have superior authority and are trying to lead the Corinthians back into the bondage of the Mosaic Law in order to have control over their lives. Paul had not tried to dominate those he taught. He writes, with irony, that he is *too weak for that*. The Christians of Corinth were being taken advantage of, financially and otherwise. The question of integrity with regard to financial matters is important because...

> Nothing exasperates God so much as embezzlement and extortion. Why? Because it is very easy to abstain from this sin. This sin springs not from natural desire that perturbs the mind, but from willful negligence...The passion of desire was implanted in our nature for the procreation of children, and anger for the succor of the injured, but love of money serves no purpose. So if you are made captive by it, you will suffer the vilest punishment. CHRYSOSTOM[3]

To steal or cheat or in any way make the acquisition of money or material goods our primary goal in life is to make money our god. Therefore, the love of money is called the *root of all kinds of evil* (1 Tim 6:10). If we allow a false god to take control of our lives, we open ourselves to unending misery.

> Let us make a comparison and see which is the more imperious, the desire of money or of beauty; for that which shall be found to have struck down great men is the more difficult to master. Let us see then what great man the desire of money ever got possession of. Not one; only of exceedingly pitiful and abject persons, Gehazi, Ahab, Judas, the priests of the Jews: but the desire for beauty overcame even the great prophet David.
>
> CHRYSOSTOM[4]

FOOD FOR THOUGHT: (b). Since sexual desire is inate and hard to resist, should sexual sins be taken lightly? (c). If love of money is easier to control, why do so many succumb to it?

11:22. Are they Hebrews? So am I. Are they Israelites? So am I. Are they the seed of Abraham? So am I. Paul's detractors assert that they have superior lineage, but there is nothing lacking in his background. Not only is he is of Hebrew heritage as they are, but also an "Israelite," the title reserved for those Jews dedicated to God. That title now belongs to those who recognize Christ as the awaited Messiah (Rom 9:6-8). Under the Blood Covenant, the "seed of Abraham" are those who belong to Christ (Gal 3:29), not those who happen to be Jews by accident of birth.

> If we, because of our faith in Christ, are deemed children of Abraham, the Jews, therefore, because of their violation of the promise have ceased to be His seed. In that fearful day when men shall be judged, good parents shall avail nothing to wicked children, as the prophet Ezekiel says (Ez 14:14). And good children will avail nothing to evil parents; rather will the goodness of their children increase the guilt of the parents (Lk 11:19).
>
> GREGORY THE GREAT[5]

11:23. Are they ministers of Christ?—I speak as a fool—I am more: in labors more abundant, in stripes above measure, in prisons more frequently, in deaths often. Paul had battle scars to prove his Apostleship. He had endured all types of affliction and faced danger of imminent death many times. He could have avoided all of this had he forsaken his mission—but he pressed on.

11:24. From the Jews five times I received forty stripes minus one. Under Mosaic Law, he who was to be punished could be sentenced to no more than forty lashes with a whip so as not to humiliate him (Deut 25:3). It was traditional, therefore, for the judge to impose one less than forty when passing sentence to insure that in his zeal the administrator would not inadvertently deliver more than forty. Paul had received thirty-nine lashes five times from his fellow Jews.

11:25. Three times I was beaten with rods; once I was stoned; three times I was shipwrecked; a night and a day I have been in the deep; One of the methods of punishment the Roman government employed for non-citizens was to beat them *with rods*. Though a Roman citizen, supposedly protected from that treatment, Paul had endured it three times. He had also been *stoned* (Acts 14:19), the method of punishment traditionally practiced by Jews. In addition, in the course of the long, perilous journeys he undertook to preach the Gospel, he had been shipwrecked three times, once spending *a night and a day* drifting bodily in the sea.

11:26-27. in journeys often, in perils of waters, in perils of robbers, in perils of my own countrymen, in perils of the Gentiles, in perils in the city, in perils in the wilderness, in perils in the sea, in perils among false brethren; in weariness and toil, in sleeplessness often, in hunger and thirst, in fastings often, in cold and nakedness. He had the self-discipline and perseverance necessary to do that which was required of him, in spite of personal peril. His missionary journeys were treacherous, without adequate food, clothing and shelter, and he faced the wrath of both Jews and Gentiles. In addition, he fasted regularly for the spiritual strength it provided. Sensing vulnerability—as he had when Christ was hungry (Mt 4:2-3)—the Devil bombarded Paul with trials and tribulations.

> Some involved labor, others sorrow, others fear, others pain, others care, others shame, others all these at once; yet he was victorious in all. And as if a single soldier, having the whole world fighting against him, should move through the ranks of his enemies and suffer no harm, so did Paul, showing himself alone among barbarians, among Greeks, on every land, on every sea,

> abide unconquered. And as a spark that changes into fire the things it touches, so did this man, setting upon all, make things change over to the truth. CHRYSOSTOM[6]

If we bear Satan's darts nobly, without giving up the struggle, the strength of the weapon is turned against that ancient enemy.

> This is the brilliant victory, this is the Church's trophy, thus is the Devil overthrown when we suffer injury. For when we suffer, he is taken captive; and himself suffers harm, when he would with joy inflict it on us. This is what happened in Paul's case; the more Satan plied him with perils, the more he was defeated. CHRYSOSTOM[7]

11:28. besides the other things, what comes upon me daily: my deep concern for all the churches. Paul had started on the road to Damascus as a persecutor and had become the persecuted. In addition to the physical and emotional ordeals he endured, He carried the weighty burden of concern for the spiritual condition of the new Christians in the areas to which he had brought the Gospel. Those who sometimes feel weighed down by worry about the spiritual condition of their own families, friends, or communities can perhaps begin to understand the immensity of the responsibility Paul felt.

11:29. Who is weak, and I am not weak? Who is made to stumble, and I do not burn with indignation? He feels the pains of his spiritual children. When some show weakness, he himself feels weak. When some are led astray, he is outraged.

11:30. If I must boast, I will boast in the things which concern my infirmity. He allows himself to boast only about those things some may consider signs of weakness: his personal involvement with his spiritual children and the suffering he has endured.

11:31. The God and Father of our Lord Jesus Christ, who is blessed forever, knows that I am not lying. He rests his case with his acknowledgement that, in the final analysis, God will judge who is speaking and living the Truth and who is not. This is the ultimate consolation for those who have done their best and are content to leave their fate in God's hands.

11:32-33. In Damascus the governor, under Aretas the king, was guarding the city of the Damascenes with a garrison, desiring to apprehend me; but I was let down in a basket through a window in the wall, and escaped from his hands. Paul reminisces about an event which occurred soon after his conversion (Acts 9:23-25), perhaps as an example of his "infirmities," the human frailties he had to struggle with daily in spite of having been chosen by God to do His work. When on his way to Damascus to continue his persecution of Christians—thinking he was doing God's will—he had experienced the very dramatic supernatural intervention of Christ, Who showed him the error of his ways. Later he fled that city and the enemies of the Gospel in a very human, even undignified manner. Those two events seem to have set the pattern for a ministry which brought him both extremes: the agony of every type of hardship imaginable and the blessed joy of being in the presence of God.

> **FOOD FOR THOUGHT:** (d). We have addressed the fact that trying to live the Christ-like life God expects of His people will inevitably bring some degree of suffering. But the suffering Paul endured was especially extensive—why?

CHAPTER ELEVEN
Food for Thought Comments

11(a). Why does God allow Satan and his followers to practice deceit?

God allows Satan to use his wiles against man as part of the sorting process necessary to single out those who belong to the Kingdom of Heaven. However, He also arms His people with knowledge of His word. He advises that they examine every person and situation in the light of that knowledge to see *whether they are of God* (1 Jn 4:1) and that they pray for guidance and discernment to avoid error. Those who follow this pattern will not be deceived.

11(b). Since sexual desire is innate and hard to resist, should sexual sins be taken lightly?

Scripture clearly indicates that sexual misconduct among Christians is not to be taken lightly. David's sinful conduct with Bathsheba "displeased the Lord" (2 Sam 11:27). Paul reacted rigorously against the man in Corinth who was involved in a sexual relationship with his stepmother (1 Cor 5:1) and against all sexual immorality in general (1 Cor 6:9). Sexual desire was given to man by God to create loving, nurturing families. This beautiful gift should not be misused.

> I say that the desire for beauty is more difficult to master than the love of money, not as extending forgiveness to those who are conquered by lust, but rather, as preparing them to be watchful. CHRYSOSTOM[8]

God created man in His image, with the ability to control passions and channel them in the right direction, unlike animals.

> God did not abolish all desire, only that which is unlawful, for He said: *let every man have his own wife, and let each woman have her own husband* (1 Cor 7:2).
> CHRYSOSTOM[9]

11(c). If love of money is easier to control than sexual desire, why do so many succumb to it?

Many are brought down by the love of money because they do not understand its dangers.

> They stand not so much on their guard against it as against promiscuity and fornication; for if they had thought it equally dangerous, they would not, perhaps, have been made its captives. CHRYSOSTOM[10]

Also, money buys the things of the world. Though they are ultimately meaningless, these things nevertheless hold much appeal for those whom Satan has managed to distract from the elements of life that have lasting value.

11(d). We have addressed that fact that trying to live the Christ-like life God expects of His people will inevitably bring some degree of suffering. But that which Paul endured was especially extensive—why?

Paul had a pivotal, difficult mission to fulfill in bringing the Gospel to the Gentiles. He possessed total love for God and dedication to Christ, the factors which qualified him for his task but which also made him vulnerable to intensive attacks by Satan, who wanted to curtail his mission.

> The higher anyone ascends in virtue, the harder will this world bear down on him; for the more the love of the heart turns from this present life, the more the opposition of the world mounts up. Hence it is that those who strive after and do that which is good struggle under a burden of afflictions. For though they have turned away from earthly things, they are harassed with increasing tribulations. But, according to the word of the Lord, they shall bring forth fruit in patience, and after their time of tribulation they shall be received into rest above because they have borne their cross in patience.
>
> GREGORY THE GREAT[11]

Paul picked up the cross he had been given to bear and followed Christ on the road to martyrdom (Mk 8:34). His struggles bore much fruit.

> He endured *shipwreck* so he might stop the shipwreck of the world; *a day and a night he passed in the deep*, so he might draw the world up from the depths of error; he was *in weariness* that he might refresh the weary; he endured smiting that he might heal those who had been smitten by the devil; he passed his time in prisons that he might lead forth to the light those who were sitting in prison and in darkness; he was *in deaths often* so he might deliver from grievous deaths; *five times he received forty stripes save one* that he might free those inflicted by the scourge of the devil; he was *beaten with rods* that he might bring them under *the rod and the staff* of Christ (Ps 23:4); he *was stoned*, that he might deliver them from the senseless stones; he was *in the wilderness*, that he might take them out of the wilderness; *in journeying*, to stop their wanderings and open the way that leads to Heaven; he was *in perils in the cities*, so he might show the city which is above; *in hunger and thirst*, to deliver from a more grievous hunger; *in nakedness*, to clothe their unseemliness with the robe of Christ; set upon by the mob, to extricate them from the besetment of fiends; he burned, that he might quench the burning darts of the devil: *through a window was let down from the wall*, to send up from below those that lay prostrate upon the ground...What all the saints together have suffered in so many bodies, he himself endured in one.
>
> CHRYSOSTOM[12]

Paul's life stands as a reminder of the power of setting a good example. If we patiently endure the hurdles Satan puts in our path and keep our eyes on God and His Kingdom, we demonstrate faith. God blesses our efforts with His grace, and we become stronger. Those witnessing this phenomenon are strengthened in their faith also. In this way, the tribulations Satan hoped would turn us away from God in bitterness and frustration can actually bring all involved closer to Him, and turn evil to good. Though we may never find the answers to all our questions in this life, we may be sure that God is in control and will never abandon us.

Some [paths to the Lord] lead over hills and mountains, and others lead down a slope. To this He says: *Every valley shall be filled, and every mountain shall be brought low*. Some of the paths are uneven, here they rise up, there they drop down; and they also are dangerous. To this He adds: *And the crooked shall be made straight and the rough ways plain*. This is accomplished spiritually, through the power of the Savior. Before, the way of evangelical belief and living was difficult because worldly pleasures bore heavily on the minds of all men. But God, made man, *has condemned sin in the flesh* (Rom 8:3), and all things have become straight, unimpeded and easy to this end; nor will hill or valley now stand in the way of those who wish to go forward.

CYRIL OF ALEXANDRIA[13]

CHAPTER TWELVE

What the Unenlightened Cannot See

BACKGROUND: Paul has shared many insights into the power and glory of God. Now he expands upon the mysteries of that which surrounds the Creator—His Kingdom.

12:1. It is doubtless not profitable for me to boast. I will come to visions and revelations of the Lord: Paul is about to relate a supernatural experience that he would normally not share with anyone because of the dangers of falling to the sin of pride. He does so now only to a limited degree, to establish, without a doubt, his authority as an Apostle.

12:2-3. I know a man in Christ who fourteen years ago—whether in the body I do not know, or whether out of the body I do not know, God knows—such a one was caught up to the third Heaven. And I know such a man—whether in the body or out of the body I do not know, God knows— He begins the tale as though it had happened to someone else. But he would not worry about seeming to boast unless referring to himself.

Around 41 AD, after his escape from Damascus but before he began his missionary journeys, Paul was transported to the "third Heaven," a Hebrew expression for the immediate presence of God. During this experience God revealed great mysteries to him, but even he did not know whether he was in his body or out of it at the time.

> Such a person does not see by sense perception, but his vision is as clear as or clearer than that by which sight perceives sensibilia. He sees by going out of himself, for through the mysterious sweetness of his vision he is ravished beyond all objects and all objective thought, and even beyond himself. GREGORY PALAMAS[1]

God gave Paul this experience because he was chosen for his ministry after Christ had ascended, so had not been taught by Him in person.

> ... that he might not seem to be inferior to the rest of the Apostles. For since they had companied with Christ, but Paul had not: He therefore caught him up unto glory also. CHRYSOSTOM[2]

12:4. how he was caught up into Paradise and heard inexpressible words, which it is not lawful for a man to utter. Paul speaks of having heard that which he could not reveal, as St. John was not allowed to write what the seven thunders had uttered (Rev 10:4). As Jesus told Nicodemus (Jn 3:12), God does not reveal His mysteries to the worldly man because they are beyond his comprehension.

> These mysteries cannot be fully known (or, rather, experienced) except by the saints—by those who live in perfect union with God, transformed by grace and belonging rather to the future life than to our earthly life.[3]

12:5-6. Of such a one I will boast; yet of myself I will not boast, except in my infirmities. For though I might desire to boast, I will not be a fool; for I will speak the truth. But I forbear, lest anyone should think of me above what he sees me to be or hears from me. Because he had this experience by "going out of himself," by being taken "beyond himself," Paul could refer to it as having happened to someone else. He resists the temptation to embellish facts to bring glory to himself, relating only that which is necessary to establish his right to try to guide the Corinthian Christians. He wants to lead them to worship God, not him.

12:7. And lest I should be exalted above measure by the abundance of the revelations, a thorn in the flesh was given to me, a messenger of Satan to buffet me, lest I be exalted above measure. The visions and revelations Paul experienced gave him spiritual wisdom and power. But the difficulties that God allowed Satan to bring to his life would remind him and all who would learn of his life and work that he was a human being, as dependent upon God as everyone else.

> Affliction rends pride away and prunes out all listlessness and exercises unto patience: it reveals the meanness of human things and leads unto much philosophy. For all the passions give way before it: anger, envy, emulation, lust, rule, desires of riches, of beauty, boastfulness, pride, anger and the whole remaining swarm of these distempers.
>
> ...For thus has God led all the saints through affliction and distress, at once doing them service and assuring that mankind will not entertain a higher opinion of them than they deserve. For thus it was that idolatries gained ground at first; men being held in admiration beyond what they deserve. CHRYSOSTOM[4]

As we learn in the story of Job, the Devil cannot touch God's people without permission from Him. God will not let us be tempted beyond what we are able to endure (I Cor 10:13).

> It is noteworthy that Satan does not claim for himself the power to strike, he who never fails to proclaim his presumption against the Author of all things. The Devil knows that by himself he is able to do nothing, for he does not even exist by himself as a spirit. It must be known that the will of Satan is always evil, but his power is never unrighteous: for his will comes from himself, but his power from God. That which he wills to do in his malice, God in His righteousness allows him to accomplish. We must not fear him who can do nothing without permission. That Power alone is to be feared Who, by allowing the Enemy to be unleashed, makes his unrighteous will serve for the execution of righteous judgments. GREGORY THE GREAT[5]

Modern theologians contend that Paul's "thorn in the flesh" was a physical malady, perhaps an affliction of the eyes that caused unsightly scaling and made looking at him unpleasant. This could account for his large handwriting (Gal 6:11) and shed light on his comment that his followers were willing to pluck out their own eyes if they could give them to him (Gal 4:13-15). An ancient theory is that Paul's problem was debilitating headaches, perhaps brought on by some type of chronic fever that attacked him repeatedly. Chrysostom, however, and most of the Greek Fathers, as well as some eminent scholars of later ages, assert that this thorn was his vulnerability to his enemies: those who tried to thwart his work and had him beaten, imprisoned and living under the constant threat of death.

12:8-9. Concerning this thing I pleaded with the Lord three times that it might depart from me. And He said to me, "My grace is sufficient for you, for My strength is made perfect in weakness." Therefore most gladly I will rather boast in my infirmities, that the power of Christ may rest upon me. When it is evident that someone has been able to accomplish a great deal in terms of doing God's work in spite of personal difficulties and shortcomings, it is clear that God's power was involved. Paul pleaded for God to deliver him from his torment but was told that this "thorn" would remain with him so it would be clear that he could not have accomplished what he did without divine assistance.

When Paul was in prison, he converted his captors (Acts 16:23-33). Time and again he overcame his persecutors (2 Cor 1:9-10, 11:23-33). He repeatedly found himself in precarious situations over which, through the grace of God, he prevailed. Although his personal suffering was intense, he knew it was a small price to pay for the power of God that was working through him.

> Knowing, then, these things, let us not fear to suffer evil, but to do evil. CHRYSOSTOM[6]

> **FOOD FOR THOUGHT:** (a). In what way are these verses important to all Christians?

12:10. Therefore I take pleasure in infirmities, in reproaches, in needs, in persecutions, in distresses, for Christ's sake. For when I am weak, then I am strong. He takes pleasure in his awareness of those areas in which he is vulnerable because he has learned that when he has done all he can do in any situation, God steps in.

> And so it was too in the Old Testament; by their trials the righteous flourished. So it was with the three children, with Daniel, with Moses, and with Joseph; they all shone and were counted worthy of great crowns. For when the soul is afflicted for God's sake, it also is purified. It receives greater assistance from God because it needs more help and is worthy of more grace. Becoming philosophic, it reaps a rich harvest of good things even before the reward which is promised to it by God.
>
> CHRYSOSTOM[7]

FOOD FOR THOUGHT: (b). Since righteous suffering can bring purification, strength, wisdom and other blessings to Christians, should we intentionally seek to suffer?

12:11-13. I have become a fool in boasting; you have compelled me. For I ought to have been commended by you; for in nothing was I behind the most eminent Apostles, though I am nothing. Truly the signs of an apostle were accomplished among you with all perseverance, in signs and wonders and mighty deeds. For what is it in which you were inferior to other churches, except that I myself was not burdensome to you? Forgive me this wrong! Paul regrets that he has been forced to defend himself and his authority. The Corinthians had witnessed many miracles that God had performed among them through him, and they were well aware of the fact that he asked for nothing for himself but their love and trust. They had benefited from his ministry and should be quick to praise him.

12:14. Now for the third time I am ready to come to you. And I will not be burdensome to you; for I do not seek yours, but you. For the children ought not to lay up for the parents but the parents for the children. He is planning to return to them soon. As in the past, he will expect nothing from them for himself. As their spiritual father, he seeks only their souls for God's Kingdom.

12:15. And I will very gladly spend and be spent for your souls; though the more abundantly I love you, the less I am loved. He will gladly give not only what he has but also of his very being out of love for them, but the more he extends himself for them, the more they seem to take him for granted. They do not reciprocate his love by defending him to his enemies.

The lack of love among Christians that this type of behavior demonstrates is very detrimental in the Church. Chrysostom wrote that under such conditions:

> I behold the mass of the Church prostrate, as though it were a corpse. And as in a body newly dead, one may see eyes and hands and feet and neck and head and yet no one limb performing its proper function; so, truly, here also, all who are here are of the faithful, but their faith is not active; for we have quenched its warmth and made the body of Christ a corpse. Now if this sounds awful when said, it is much more awful when it appears in actions. For we have indeed the name of brothers but do the deeds of foes; and while all are called members, we are divided against each other like wild beasts. I have said this not from a desire to parade our condition but to shame you and make you desist. Such and such a man goes into a house; honor is paid to him; you ought to give God thanks because your member is honored and God is glorified; but you do the contrary: you speak evil of him to the man that honored him, so that you trip up the heels of both and besides, disgrace yourself. And why, wretched and miserable one? Have you heard your brother praised, either among men or women? Add to his praises, for so you shall praise yourself also. But if you overthrow the praise, first you have spoken evil of yourself, having so acquired an ill character, and you have raised him the higher. When you hear one praised, become a partner in what is said; if not in your life and virtue, yet still in rejoicing over his excellencies. Do you see what disgrace we are the causes of to ourselves? How we destroy and rend the flock? Let us at length be members (of one another), let us become one body.
>
> CHRYSOSTOM[8]

12:16-19. But be that as it may, I did not burden you. Nevertheless, being crafty, I caught you with guile! Did I take advantage of you by any of those whom I sent to you? I

urged Titus, and sent our brother with him. Did Titus take advantage of you? Did we not walk in the same spirit? Did we not walk in the same steps? Again, do you think that we excuse ourselves to you? We speak before God in Christ. But we do all things, beloved, for your edification. Paul received no earthly benefit for himself for his work with the Corinthians. Neither did he arrange to be compensated through those he sent to continue the work. Their purpose was to bring the light of the Gospel to the Corinthians—nothing else. The money they have collected is for the saints in Jerusalem, not for him.

12:20-21. For I fear lest, when I come, I shall not find you such as I wish, and that I shall be found by you such as you do not wish; lest there be contentions, jealousies, outbursts of wrath, selfish ambitions, backbitings, whisperings, conceits, tumults; and lest, when I come again, my God will humble me among you, and I shall mourn for many who have sinned before and have not repented of the uncleanness, fornication, and licentiousness which they have practiced. Paul's fear is that his desire to present the church in Corinth to Christ unblemished will not be realized—that he will find it defiled by sin.

> It is not enough to read and to study the sacred Scriptures, we must fulfill them also. To me it seems that if anyone is involved in contentions and in quarrels, his prayers are not acceptable, his supplications are not answered, his gift rises not upwards from the earth; and neither does the giving of alms avail him for the forgiveness of his sins. And wheresoever there is no peace and tranquility, the door is left open to the Evil One.
>
> APHRAATES[9]

His hope is that he will find that the Corinthian Christians have repented, so he can guide them to the glories of continued spiritual growth.

> To repent means both to lament the sins we have committed and to refrain from the sins we lament. For the one who grieves over some sins yet continues to commit others either does not know how to repent or but pretends to repent.
>
> GREGORY THE GREAT[10]

CHAPTER TWELVE
Food for Thought Comments

12(a). In what way is 2 Cor 12:8-9 important to all Christians?

There has never been, nor will there ever be, a person who has not had some difficulty to deal with in life. Thus the fact that the exact nature of Paul's affliction is a matter of conjecture is an advantage. Shrouded in mystery, it stands as a source of strength for everyone, for no one can say that it was less difficult than what s/he has had to endure. When, in spite of physical infirmities or difficult situations in our lives, we *press toward the goal* of trying to become Christ-like (Phil 3:14), we demonstrate the power and glory of God and His divine plan. It is easy to say we love God when all is well in our lives and in the lives of those we love. Adversities test our faith. Satan refused to believe Job's faith in God was real while he had family, friends, wealth, and health (Job 1:7-12 & 2:1-6). When God allowed Satan to take everything from Job, finally including his health, to test his faith and love and still he remained steadfast, everything was restored to him twice-over (Job 42: 1-10).

> If then you are a disciple, travel the straight and narrow way, and be not disgusted nor discouraged. For even if you are not afflicted in one way, you must inevitably be afflicted in another. For the envious man, the lover of money, he that burns for a harlot, the vainglorious and everyone who follows what is evil endures many disheartenings and afflictions and is not less afflicted than the true Christian...Since then whether we follow this way of life or that, we will be afflicted: why not choose the way which along with affliction brings crowns innumerable? CHRYSOSTOM[11]

12(b). Since righteous suffering can bring purification, strength, wisdom and other blessings to Christians, should we intentionally seek to suffer?

When the early Christians began to realize that there were blessings inherent in righteous suffering, some began to go out of their way to put themselves in situations which would bring pain. But contrived or self-inflicted agony is useless. We do not have the right to inflict suffering upon ourselves or others, nor should we seek it as an end unto itself—it will find us soon enough. Paul's example tells us to do all we can, short of denying Christ or compromising our faith, to avoid such situations and to keep ourselves strong for the work the Lord has for us to do. However, if suffering plants itself firmly in our lives, we should pray for God's help and while keeping our eyes on Him, do what we can to help ourselves. If we hang on and carry on, He will do the rest—He will see us through. When addressing the possibility of facing persecution, Scripture is clearly against self-surrender:

> *You will be hated by all for My name's sake. But he who endures to the end will be saved. But when they persecute you in this city, flee to another* (Mt 10: 22-23).

Polycarp was the Bishop of Smyrna for much of the first half of the second century. When he was about eighty-six years of age, he was urged to pay homage to Caesar and recognize him as "Lord." To a Christian, this was to deny Christ. Polycarp refused, so was tied to a pyre and set aflame. Marcion was an eye witness to the martyrdom of this saintly man. He wrote in glowing terms about the courage and joy with which Polycarp faced death at the hands of his persecutors.

Marcion also wrote about another incident which occurred when courage failed a Christian who deliberately put himself in harm's way.

> There was one man...Quintus by name, a Phrygian recently arrived from Phrygia, whose courage failed him at the sight of the beasts. It was he who had compelled himself and some others to surrender themselves voluntarily; and after much persuasion he was induced to take the oath and offer incense.[12] (And that is the reason, brothers, why we do not approve of men offering themselves spontaneously. We are not taught anything of that kind in the Gospel.) MARCION[13]

CHAPTER THIRTEEN
With Paternal Regard

BACKGROUND: Paul's tender affection toward the Christians of Corinth, his spiritual children, has been evident throughout his two epistles to them. Like a concerned father, he has continuously admonished them about their transgressions and postponed his next visit to give them ample time to change their ways before his arrival. In this final chapter, he makes it clear that this time has run out.

13:1-2. This will be the third time I am coming to you. "By the mouth of two or three witnesses every word shall be established." I have told you before and foretell as if I were present the second time, and now being absent I write to those who have sinned before, and to all the rest, that if I come again I will not spare—When Paul returns to Corinth he will deal with those in the church who continue to live sinfully. He quotes Deut 19:15, the Old Testament standard for establishing guilt.

13:3-4. since you seek a proof of Christ speaking in me, who is not weak toward you, but mighty in you. For though He was crucified in weakness, yet He lives by the power of God. For we also are weak in Him, but we shall live with Him by the power of God toward you. The boldness and strength they will see in him during his next visit stem from his authority through Christ. His reluctance to display this power in the past was not due to weakness. On the contrary, it was proof of his strengths of patience and love. The human weakness he has displayed, his vulnerability to persecution from his enemies, was the same weakness that Christ endured. But Christ's willingness to endure the limitations of the human body, which put Him under the physical power of His enemies, was actually a sign of His strength.

> *Because the foolishness of God is wiser than men, and the weakness of God is stronger than men* (1 Cor 1:25).

> There is no real weakness or foolishness in God. Away with the thought! For that He had it in His power not to have been crucified He showed throughout; when He cast men down prostrate, turned back the beams of the sun, withered a fig tree, blinded their eyes that came against Him and wrought ten thousand other things. What then is this which he says, *in weakness*! That even though He was crucified after enduring peril and treachery...yet still He was not harmed.
>
> CHRYSOSTOM[1]

13:5-6. Examine yourselves as to whether you are in the faith. Prove yourselves. Do you not know yourselves, that Jesus Christ is in you?—unless indeed you are disqualified. But I trust that you will know that we are not disqualified. Paul asks that they assess their lives to see whether they really show signs of faith. We are a part of Christ through Baptism and Eucharist and remain so as long as we try to live Christ-like lives. If we do not participate in this struggle through all the situations of life, we disqualify ourselves from God's Kingdom, just as those who participate in any quest are subject to the conditions involved.

> **FOOD FOR THOUGHT:** (a). What is the message of verses 5-6 to the modern Christian?

13:7. Now I pray to God that you do no evil, not that we should appear approved, but that you should do what is honorable, though we may seem disqualified. His prayer is that they not cut themselves off from communion with God. He would rather that all his concerns seem unfounded and his threats foolish than that he find them in spiritual decay.

13:8. For we can do nothing against the truth, but for the truth. His spiritual power stems from his faith in the truths God has revealed to those who love Him. If Paul were to act outside these truths, he would find himself powerless.

> **FOOD FOR THOUGHT:** (b). What special power did Paul and the Apostles have in the early Church?

13:9-10. For we are glad when we are weak and you are strong. And this also we pray, that you may be made complete. Therefore I write these things being absent, lest being present I should use sharpness, according to the authority which the Lord has given me for edification and not for destruction. To find them spiritually strong and healthy would make him happy but leave him without the power that is his when he has to battle ungodliness. But he would rather be thought weak than have to take measures against them. He would rather be severe in his letters to them than in actions toward them. The authority God gave him was to build up the Church—not destroy it.

13:11. Finally, brethren, farewell. Paul has done all that he can. He has taught them the fullness of the Gospel, pointed out the areas in which they have been disobedient and outlined the present and eternal consequences if they do not change their ways. The rest is up to them. His final words are those of an affectionate father:

Become complete...amend your lives—make whatever changes are necessary to be in communion with God.

be of good comfort...take comfort from one another, from God's word and His promises, and from a clear conscience.

be of one mind and live in peace; be united, not only about doctrine but in day-to-day dealings with one another and with God's creation.

> While you are on earth, regard yourself as a guest of the Host, that is, of Christ. If you are at table, He honors you thus. If you breathe the air, you breathe His air. If you bathe, you bathe in His water. If you travel, you travel around His earth. If you accumulate goods, you accumulate what is His; if you squander them, you squander what is His. If you are influential, you are so by His permission. If you are in company with others, you are with His other guests. If you are in the countryside, you are in His garden. If you are alone, He is present. If you set off anywhere, He sees you. If you do anything, He

has it in mind. He is the most careful Host Whose guest you have ever been. And be, in your turn, careful towards Him. A good host merits a good guest.[2]

and the God of love and peace will be with you. To live in accordance with God's plan for man is to know unparalleled love and peace. When we are right with our Maker, we know it, we feel it. His love is sweet.

> *Taste and see that the Lord is good, Blessed is the man who trusts in Him* (Ps 34:8)!

> **FOOD FOR THOUGHT:** (c). How does Paul's paternal approach to the Corinthians follow the pattern of God's dealings with mankind?

13:12. Greet one another with a holy kiss. As in the closing of the First Epistle to the Corinthians, Paul refers to the holy kiss. It is a pious tradition within Orthodoxy to greet one another in this way, as the early Christians did, as a symbol of the love Christ said we should have for one another as members of the Body of Christ (Jn 15:12).

> What is *holy*? Not hollow, not treacherous, like the kiss Judas gave to Christ. The kiss is given that it may be fuel unto love, that it may kindle the disposition, that we may so love each other, as brothers brothers, as children parents, as parents children, but even far more. For those things are implanted by nature, but these by spiritual grace.
>
> ...We are the temple of Christ; we kiss the porch and entrance of the temple when we kiss each other...And through these gates and doors Christ both had entered into us, and does enter, whenever we commune. You who partake of the Mysteries understand what I say. For it is in no common manner that our lips are honored, when they receive the Lord's Body. It is for this reason chiefly that we here kiss. Pay attention—those who speak filthy things, who swear, and let them shudder to think what that mouth is they dishonor. CHRYSOSTOM[3]

The holy kiss found expression in the ancient celebration of the Divine Liturgy. Just before the recitation of the Creed, the Kiss of Peace was exchanged by all in attendance, signifying unity in faith. In modern times, this beautiful practice is often eliminated, except among the clergy when more than one priest co-celebrates. Some parishes have revived this meaningful practice, allowing the faithful the opportunity to express their love for one another as fellow travelers on the road to union with God. This type of love is powerful, capable of manifesting itself even among strangers.

> We forget that in the call to "greet one another with a holy kiss" we are talking not of our personal, natural, human love, through which we cannot in fact love someone who is a "stranger," who has not yet become "something" or "somebody" for us, but of the *love of Christ*, the eternal wonder of which consists precisely in the fact that it transforms the *stranger* (and each stranger, in his depths, is an *enemy*) into a *brother*, irrespective of whether he has or does not have relevance for me and for my life; that it is the very purpose of the Church to overcome the horrible *alienation* that was introduced into the world by the Devil and proved to be its undoing. And we forget that we come to church for this love, which is always granted to us in the gathering of the brethren.[4]

13:13. All the saints greet you. This greeting from the "saints," the other Christians with Paul, is a reminder of the universal Church. All who worship in Truth and try to live accordingly are united in love through Christ. Together they make up the Body of Christ and thus are saints.

13:14. The grace of the Lord Jesus Christ, and the love of God, and the communion of the Holy Spirit be with you all. Amen. With this invocation of the Holy Trinity, Paul reaches out to all, through the ages, who read this epistle. These powerful words have come to be known as the Apostolic Benediction, with which Orthodox priests bless worshippers during the Divine Liturgy.

Paul did, finally, return to Corinth. He spent the winter there as he had hoped (1 Cor 16:5,6). It was during this time that he wrote his Epistle to the Romans (c.57 A.D.).

CHAPTER THIRTEEN
Food for Thought Comments

13(a). What is the message of 2 Cor 13:5-6 to the modern Christian?

Christ does not remain with those who live in disobedience. Those who partake of Eucharist without sincerely attempting to rid themselves of the corruption of sin receive condemnation rather than blessing (1 Cor 11:27-30). To live long, healthy, productive lives on earth we must continually assess our physical state and do what is necessary to remain in optimal condition. To live eternally with God, it is even more important that we apply this principle to our spiritual condition.

13(b). What special power did Paul and the Apostles have in the early Church?

The Apostles were occasionally the vehicles through which consequences of sin took physical effect immediately, as with Ananias and Sapphira (Acts 5:1-10) and Elymas (Acts 13:6-11). These actions were aimed at teaching those involved, and those looking on, that disobedience to God carries consequences (see Acts 5:11 and Acts 13:12). Paul and the Apostles also had the spiritual powers that Priests of today have to bind sin (Jn 20:23) and to deny access to the Sacraments of the Church (1 Cor 5:3-5).

13(c). How does Paul's paternal approach to the Corinthians follow the pattern of God's dealings with mankind?

A good father makes certain his children know what he expects of them for their own good and gives them every opportunity to grow in that direction. He assists them along the way, as Paul helped the Corinthians, but then follows through with stated consequences if his instructions are not heeded, in order to prevent their falling into harm. This is what God has done with man. He has made His divine plan for His Kingdom known through Scripture. These writings teach, explain and warn of the consequences of indifference to or disobedience of these precepts. He allows ample time for all to learn, to repent, and to try to comply, but the allotted time will run out. At the Second Coming of Christ, which will occur at a time known by no one, judgment will take place:

> All the nations will be gathered before Him, and He will separate them one from another as a shepherd divides his sheep from the goats. And He will set the sheep on His right hand, but the goats on the left. Then the King will say to those at His right hand, *"Come, you blessed of My Father, inherit the kingdom prepared for you from the foundation of the world;"* Then He will say to those on the left hand, *"Depart from Me, you cursed, into the everlasting fire prepared for the devil and his angels "* (Mt. 25:32-34,41).

> Let us then continue to hold these doctrines in their strictness and to draw to us the love of God. For before indeed He loved us when hating Him and reconciled us who were His enemies; but henceforth He wishes to love us as loving Him. Let us then continue to love Him, so that we may also be loved by Him. For if when beloved by powerful men we are formidable to all, much more when beloved by God. And should it be needful to give wealth, or body, or even life itself for this love, let us not grudge them. It is not enough to say in words that we love, we ought to give also the proof of deeds; for neither did He show love by words only, but by deeds also. Do then also show Him by deeds and do those things which please Him for so shall you reap the advantage. For He needs nothing that we have to bestow, and this is also special proof of a sincere love, when one Who needs nothing does all for the sake of being loved by us. *For what does the Lord God require of you, but to love Him, and that you should be ready to walk after Him* (Deut 10:12)?
>
> CHRYSOSTOM[5]

Amen.

Notes

Chapter One

1. M. F. Toal, "What is Peace," *Sunday Sermons of the Great Fathers,* Vol. Three, p.39.

2. Philip Schaff, "Homily I on Second Corinthians," *The Nicene and Post-Nicene Fathers of the Christian Church*, Vol. XII, *Chrysostom: Homilies on the Epistles of Paul to the Corinthians,* p.275.

3. ibid, p.274.

4. ibid, "Homily III," p.292.

5. ibid, "Homily II," p.279.

6. Toal, "On Prayer," Vol. Two, p.396.

7. ibid, p.389.

8. ibid, "That Prayer is to be Placed before all Things," p.380.

9. Schaff, "Homily III," Vol. XII, p.286.

10. Vladimir Lossky, *In the Image and Likeness of God,* p.59.

11. Philip Schaff and Henry Wace, "Letter CCXXXIII," *NPNF*, Second Series, Vol. VIII, *St. Basil: Letters and Select Works*, p.273.

12. ibid, "Letter XI. Easter, 339," Vol. IV, *Select Works and Letters* p.536.

13. Toal, "On the Holy Pasch II," Vol. Two, p.249.

14. ibid, "On the Gospel," Vol. One, p.417.

15. Bishop Nikolai Velimirovic, *The Prologue from Ochrid, Lives of the Saints and Homilies for Every Day in the Year*, Part One, p.332.

16. Roberts and Donaldson, "Against Heresies," *The Ante-Nicene Fathers, Writings of the Fathers down to A.D. 325*, Vol. I, p.518.

17. Fr. Seraphim Rose, *The Place of the Blessed Augustine in the Orthodox Church,* p.9-20.

18. Vladimir Lossky, *Orthodox Theology, An Introduction*, p.72-73.

19. Vergilius Ferm, *Encyclopedia of Religion,* p.570.

20. Archimandrite Christoforos Stavropoulos, *Partakers of Divine Nature,* p.34.

21. Colm Luibheid, trans., "Conference Three," *John Cassian, Conferences,* p.93.

22. Schaff and Wace, "Against the Heathen," Vol. IV, p.6.

23. Daniel M. Rogich, *St. Gregory Palamas, Treatise on the Spiritual Life*, p.73-74.

24. Toal, "Man is Delivered by Trials: Mystical Joy," Vol. Four, p.197.

25. Schaff, "Homily I," Vol. XII, p.275.

26. Lossky, *Theology,* p.129.

27. Schaff, "Homily II on Second Corinthians," Vol. XII, p.281.

28. G.E.H. Palmer, Philip Sherrard, Kallistos Ware, "Spurious Knowledge," *The Philokalia,* Vol. Three, p.202.

29. Toal, "On Prayer," Vol. Two, p.397.

30. ibid, p.383.
31. Lossky, *Theology*, p.85.
32. Toal, "The Holy Trinity," Vol. Three, p.66.
33. ibid, "Exposition of the Gospel," p.23.
34. Schaff and Wace, "On the Spirit," Vol. VIII, p.23.
35. Toal, "The Meaning of Pentecost," Vol. Three, p.32.
36. Schaff, "Homily II," Vol. XII, p.283.
37. Toal, "On the Gospel," Vol. One, p.325.

Chapter Two

1. Schaff, "Homily IV," Vol. XII, p.296.
2. ibid, p.297.
3. ibid.
4. ibid, "Homily XV," p.354.
5. ibid, "Homily V," p.301.
6. Archbishop Averky, *Apocalypse*, p.91.
7. Palmer, Sherrard, Ware, "Love," (97), Vol. Three, p.328.
8. Schaff, "Homily VI," Vol. XII, p.308.
9. Lossky, *Theology*, p.81-82.
10. David Winter, "The Likeness of God," *Faith Under Fire*, (Day 100).
11. Schaff, "Homily IV," Vol. XII, p.297.
12. ibid, p.299.
13. ibid, p.298.
14. Toal, "The Eucharist in Prophecy," Vol. Three, p.113.
15. ibid, "The Leaven of Holiness," Vol. One, p.353.
16. Roberts and Donaldson, "The Epistle of Polycarp," Vol. I, p.34.

Chapter Three

1. Chrysostom; Toal, "The Transfiguration of Christ," Vol. Two, p.54-55.
2. Philip Schaff, "Homily XXII on the Epistle to the Hebrews," *NPNF, Chrysostom: Homilies on the Gospel of St. John and the Epistle to the Hebrews,* Vol. XIV, p.467.
3. Roberts and Donaldson, "Epistle of Mathetes to Diognetus," Vol. I, p.28.

4. Lossky, *Theology*, p.86.

5. R. Payne Smith, "On the Incarnation," *Commentary on the Gospel of St. Luke*, note 1, p.52.

6. George C. Berthold, "Chapters on Knowledge," (90), *Maximus Confessor, Selected Writings*, p.145.

7. Schaff, "Homily VI on Second Corinthians," Vol. XII, p.307.

8. ibid, "Homily VII," p.310,311.

9. ibid, "Homily VI," p.307.

10. Alexander Schmemann, *The Eucharist*, p.104.

11. Schaff, "Homily IV," Vol. XII, p.299.

12. Philip Schaff, "Homily XI on the Epistle to the Romans," *NPNF*, Vol XI, p.411.

13. ibid, "Homily VII," Vol. XII, p.312.

14. ibid.

15. ibid, p.311.

16. ibid, p.312, note 4.

17. ibid, "Homily XIX on Romans," Vol. XI, p.488.

18. ibid, "Homily VII," Vol. XII, p.314.

19. Schaff and Wace, "Against the Heathen," Vol. IV, p.5.

20. Justin explains *knives of stone* as "the words preached by the Apostles of the corner-stone cut out without hands." Roberts and Donaldson, "Dialogue of Justin, Philosopher and Martyr, with Trypho, A Jew," Vol. I, p.256.

21. ibid, p.206.

22. Schmemann, p.115.

23. Rev. Stanley S. Harakas, "Capital Punishment" (39), Social Issues, Part IV, *Contemporary Moral Issues Facing the Orthodox Christian*, p.154-157.

24. Nikolaos P. Vassiliadis, *The Mystery of Death*, p.164.

25. Photios Kontoglou, Ekphrasis, p.180.

26. Toal, "On the Gospel," Vol. One, p.382.

27. Schaff, "Homily VI," Vol. XII, p.308.

28. ibid.

29. Palmer, Sherrard, Ware, "The Raising of the Intellect," (62), Vol. Three, p.312.

30. Schaff, "Homily VII," Vol. XII, p.314.

Chapter Four

1. Archimandrite Chrysostomos, *The Ancient Fathers of the Desert*, p.66.
2. Palmer, Sherrard, Ware, "The Freedom of the Intellect," (143), Vol. Three, p.350.
3. Berthold, "Four Hundred Chapters on Love" (55), p.81.
4. Schaff and Wace, "Against the Heathen," Vol. IV, p.5.
5. Palmer, Sherrard, Ware, "The Freedom of the Intellect," (149), Vol. Three, p.353.
6. Roberts and Donaldson, "The Epistle to Diognetus," Vol. I, p.27-28.
7. Toal, "Prayer for the Future Life," Vol. Four, p.347.
8. Schaff, "Homily IX on Second Corinthians," Vol. XII, p.322.
9. ibid, "Homily VII," p.317.
10. ibid, "Homily IX," p.325.
11. Schaff and Wace, "Against the Heathen," Vol. IV, p.6.
12. Toal, "The Leaven of Holiness," Vol. One, p.355.
13. ibid, "The First Sunday of Lent," Vol. Two, p.6.
14. ibid, "Man is Delivered by Trials: Mystical Joy," Vol. Four, p.198.
15. ibid, "First Sunday of Lent," Vol. Two, p.4.
16. Schaff and Wace, "The Hexaemeron," Vol. VIII, p.78.
17. Toal, "Prayer for the Future Life," Vol. Four, p.347.

Chapter Five

1. Roberts and Donaldson, "Fragments of the Lost Work of Justin on the Resurrection," Vol. I, p.297.
2. Chrysostom; Schaff, "Homily X," Vol. XII, p.327.
3. Philip Schaff and Henry Wace, "Lecture IV" (30), *NPNF*, Second Series, Vol. VII, *St. Cyril of Jerusalem, St. Gregory Nazianzen*, p.26.
4. Toal, "On the Consolation of Death, Second Sermon," Vol. Four, p.360.
5. Roberts & Donaldson, "Fragments from the Lost Writings of Irenaeus," Vol. I, p.570.
6. Schaff and Wace, "Lecture XV," (23 and 25), Vol. VII, p.111,112.
7. Panayiotis Nellas, "Garments of Skin," *Deification in Christ*, p.46-53.
8. Lossky, *Image*, p.222.
9. Roberts and Donaldson, "Against Heresies," Vol. I, p.540.

10. ibid, p.531.
11. Toal, "On the Consolation of Death, First Sermon," Vol. Four, p.318.
12. Lossky, *Theology*, p.83.
13. ibid, p.113.
14. ibid, p.92.
15. Toal, "On the Consolation of Death, First Sermon," Vol. Four, p.318.
16. ibid, "The Leaven of Holiness," Vol. One, p.354.
17. Maxwell Staniforth, "The Blessedness of Christian Love," (49), *Early Christian Writings, The Apostolic Fathers*, p.49.
18. ibid, (50), p.49.
19. Schaff, "Homily XI on Second Corinthians," Vol. XII, p.333.
20. Timothy Ware, *The Orthodox Church*, p.279.
21. Winter, "The Difference," (Day 5).
22. Lossky, *Image*, p.97.
23. Schaff and Wace, "Letter CCXXXIV," Vol. VIII, p.274.
24. John Meyendorff, "Essence and Energies in God," *Gregory Palamas, The Triads*, p.108.
25. Lossky, *Image*, p.56 and note 27.
26. Meyendorff, "The Uncreated Glory," p.88.
27. Ware, *Church*, p.68.
28. Schaff and Wace, "Letter CLXXXIX," Vol. VIII, p.231.
29. Toal, "The Resurrection of the Body," Vol. Four, p.123,125.
30. ibid, "On the Consolation of Death, Second Sermon," p.359.
31. ibid, "The Resurrection of the Body," p.126-127.
32. Kallistos Ware, *The Orthodox Way*, p.182.
33. Toal, "The Resurrection of the Body," Vol. Four, p.128.
34. Roberts and Donaldson, "Against Heresies," Vol. I, p.561.
35. ibid, "On the Resurrection," Vol. I, p.295.
36. Palmer, Sherrard, Ware, "Texts on Watchfulness," (20), Vol. Three, p.24.
37. Toal, "On the Resurrection of the Dead, Second Sermon," Vol. Four, p.386.
38. ibid, p.400-402.
39. Schaff and Wace, "Lecture XVIII," (19), Vol. VII, p.139.
40. Toal, "On the Resurrection of the Dead, Second Sermon," Vol. Four, p.395.
41. Schaff, "Homily IX on First Corinthians," Vol. XII, p.49.
42. Athanasios S. Frangopoulos, "The Completion of Redemption," *Our Orthodox Christian Faith*, p.239.
43. Schaff and Wace, "Against the Heathen," (33), Vol. IV, p.21.

44. Frangopoulos, "The Completion of all Things," p.249.
45. Palmer, Sherrard, Ware, "The Raising of the Intellect," (63), Vol. Three, p.312.
46. Schaff and Wace, "Lecture XV," (26), Vol. VII, p.112.
47. Schaff, "Homily X on Second Corinthians," Vol. XII, p.330.

Chapter Six

1. Schaff, "Homily XII on Second Corinthians," Vol XII, p.336.
2. ibid, "Homily XV," p.353.
3. ibid, "Homily XII," p.338.
4. ibid, "Homily XIV on First Corinthians," p.80.
5. ibid, "Homily XII on Second Corinthians," p.338.
6. Toal, "On Jesus Ascending to Jerusalem," Vol. One, p.414.
7. Colm Luibheid and Norman Russell, "Step 22," (On Vainglory), *John Climacus, The Ladder of Divine Ascent*, p.205.
8. Toal, "On the Mystical Church," Vol. One, p.94.
9. Schaff, "Homily XII," Vol. XII, p.339.
10. Luibheid and Russell, "Step 30," (On Faith, Hope, and Love), *Ladder*, p.288.
11. Roberts and Donaldson, "Epistle to Diognetus," Vol. I, p.29.
12. Palmer, Sherrard, Ware, "Love," Vol. Three, p.254.
13. Roberts and Donaldson, "Epistle to Diognetus," Vol. I, p.29.
14. John Cassian, "Institutes," Book XII, Chap. XXIX, *Teachings on the Spiritual Life, Selected from the Writings of St. John Cassian the Roman*, p.99.
15. Schaff, "Homily XII," Vol. XII, p.340.

Chapter Seven

1. Toal, "On the Gospel," Vol. Two, p.176.
2. Alexander Schmemann, *Great Lent, Journey to Pascha*, Appendix, p.122.
3. Toal, "On the Gospel," Vol. Two, p.22.
4. Schaff, "Homily XV," Vol. XII, p.350.
5. Palmer, Sherrard, Ware, "Treasury of Divine Knowledge," Vol. Three, p.88.
6. Schaff, "Homily XV," Vol. XII, p.352.
7. ibid, "Homily XIII," p.345.
8. Winter, "The Word, our Instructor," (Day 52).

9. Toal, "On Envy," Vol. Four, p.142.
10. Schaff, "Homily IX on Philippians," Vol. XIII, p.229.
11. Toal, "The Christian Manner of Life," Vol. Three, p.239.
12. Winter, "Helping those who Have Fallen Away" (Day 50).
13. Velimirovic, Part One, p.207.
14. Staniforth, "To Polycarp," p.127.
15. ibid, "Practical Conclusions," (10), p.181.
16. Toal, "The Leaven of Holiness," Vol. One, p.354.
17. ibid, "The Authority and Dignity of the Priesthood," Vol. Two, p.274.

Chapter Eight

1. Schaff, "Homily XVI on Second Corinthians," Vol. XII, p.357.
2. ibid, p.356.
3. Toal, "I Will Pull Down My Barns," Vol. Three, p.327.
4. Schaff, "Homily XVII," Vol. XII, p.360.
5. Toal, "Christian Moderation," Vol. One, p.400.
6. Schaff, "Homily XIX," Vol. XII, p.371.
7. ibid, "Homily XVII," p.361.
8. ibid.
9. ibid, "Homily XVI" p.358.
10. Toal, "Steps of the Ascent to Blessedness," Vol. Four, p.480.
11. Winter, "Enjoying our Possessions," (Day 21).
12. Luibheid and Russell, "Step 2," (On Detachment), *Ladder*, p.82.
13. ibid.
14. Schaff, "Homily XVII," Vol. XII, p.361.
15. Toal, "I Will Pull Down my Barns," Vol. Three, p.327.
16. ibid, "On the Love of the Poor," Vol. Four, p.56.
17. ibid, "Meditation on the Mystical Supper," Vol. Three, p.156.
18. ibid, "I Will Pull Down my Barns," p.325.
19. Schaff, "Homily XVII," Vol. XII, p.362.

Chapter Nine

1. Schaff, "Homily XVI," p.359.
2. ibid, "Homily XLIII on First Corinthians," p.262.
3. ibid, "Homily XIX on Second Corinthians," Vol. XII, p.370.
4. ibid, "Homily XX," p.374.
5. ibid.

6. Velimirovic, Part One, p.23.
7. Winter, "Deal with the Cause First," (Day 31).
8. Toal, "The Fountain of Alms," Vol. Three, p.311.

Chapter Ten

1. Palmer, Sherrard, Ware, "Texts on Watchfulness," (20), Vol. Three, p.24.
2. Stavropoulos, p.49.
3. Schaff, "Homily XXI on Second Corinthians," Vol. XII, p.376.
4. Winter, "Our Attitude to Unbelievers," (Day 25).
5. Toal, "The Tares and the Wheat," Vol. One, p.339.
6. ibid, "Meditation on the Mystery of the Word Incarnate," Vol. Four, p.167.
7. ibid, Augustine on "The Tares and the Wheat," Vol. One, p.338.
8. ibid, p.337.
9. Palmer, Sherrard and Ware, "Discrimination," Vol. Three, p.152.
10. Luibheid and Russell, "Step 25," (On Humility), *Ladder*, p.218-228.
11. Palmer, Sherrard & Ware, "True Discrimination," Vol. Three, p.158.
12. ibid, "Discrimination," p.243.
13. Luibheid and Russell, "Step 26," (On Discernment), *Ladder*, p.229.

Chapter Eleven

1. Toal, "First Sunday of Lent," Vol. Two, p.21.
2. Schaff, "Homily XXIV," Vol. XII, p.390.
3. ibid, "Homily XXIII," p.389.
4. ibid.
5. Toal, "On the Mystical Church," Vol. One, p.92.
6. Schaff, "Homily XXV," Vol. XII, p.396.
7. ibid.
8. ibid, "Homily XXIII," p.389.
9. ibid.
10. ibid, p.390.
11. Toal, "Christian Moderation," Vol. One, p.401.
12. Schaff, "Homily XXV," Vol. XII, p.397.
13. Toal, "Fourth Sunday of Advent," Vol. One, p.75.

Chapter Twelve

1. Meyendorff, p.38.
2 Schaff, "Homily XXVI on Second Corinthians," Vol. XII, p.399.
3. Lossky, *Image*, p.50.
4 Schaff, "Homily XXVI," Vol. XII, p.401-402.
5. Lossky, *Image*, p.217.
6. Schaff, "Homily XXVIII," Vol. XII, p.411.
7. ibid, "Homily XXVI, p.401.
8. ibid, "Homily XXVII," p.406.
9. Toal, "Against Discord and Anger," Vol. One, p.346.
10. ibid, "The Angelic Choirs," Vol. Three, p.210.
11. Schaff, "Homily XXVI," Vol. XII, p.402.
12. Just as the righteous of old were urged to worship pagan gods (Dan 3:15), early Christians were often given the choice of paying homage to the reigning emperor and burning incense in his honor or losing their lives through a torturous death like being fed to wild beasts.
13. Staniforth, "The Martyrdom of Polycarp," (4), p.156.

Chapter Thirteen

1. Schaff, "Homily XXIX," Vol. XII, p.414.
2. Velimirovic, Part One, p.254.
3. Schaff, "Homily XXX," Vol. XII, p.418.
4. Schmemann, *Eucharist*, p.139.
5. Schaff, "Homily XXX," Vol. XII, p.419.

Bibliography

Averky, Archbishop of Jordanville. *The Apocalypse of St. John*. Platina, CA: St. Herman of Alaska Brotherhood, 1985.

Berthold, George C., trans. *Maximus Confessor, Selected Writings*. Mahwah, NJ: Paulist Press, 1985.

Cassian, John. *Institutes, Teachings on the Spiritual Life*. Willits, CA: Eastern Orthodox Books.

Chrysostomos, Archimandrite. Trans. from the Evergetinos on Passions and Perfection in Christ, *The Ancient Fathers of the Desert*. Brookline, MA: Hellenic College Press, 1980.

Ferm, Vergilius, ed. *Encyclopedia of Religion*. New York, NY: Philosophical Library, Inc., 1981.

Frangopoulos, Athanasios. *Our Orthodox Christian Faith, A Handbook of Popular Dogmatics*. Athens: The Brotherhood of Theologians, 1984.

Harakas, Stanley S. *Contemporary Moral Issues Facing the Orthodox Christian*. Minneapolis, MN: Light & Life Publishing Co., 1982.

Kontoglou, Photios. *Ekphrasis*, 3rd ed., Vol. I. Athens: Astir Press, 1993.

Lossky, Vladimir. *In the Image and Likeness of God*. Crestwood, NY: St. Vladimir's Seminary Press, 1974.

______. *Orthodox Theology, An Introduction*. Crestwood, NY: St. Vladimir's Seminary Press, 1978.

Luibheid, Colm, trans. *John Cassian, Conferences*. Mahwah, NJ: Paulist Press, 1985.

Luibheid, Colm, and Norman Russell. *John Climacus, The Ladder of Divine Ascent*. Ramsey, NJ: Paulist Press, 1982.

Meyendorff, John, ed. *Gregory Palamas, The Triads*. Mahwah, NJ: Paulist Press, 1983.

Nellas, Panayiotis. *Deification in Christ, The Nature of the Human Person*. Crestwood, NY: St. Vladimir's Seminary Press, 1987.

Palmer, G.E.H., Philip Sherrard and Kallistos Ware, ed., *The Philokalia*. 3 vols. London and Boston, MA: Faber and Faber, Inc., 1984.

Roberts, Rev. Alexander and Donaldson, James, ed.*The Ante-Nicene Fathers, Translations of the Writings of the Fathers down to A.D. 325*. Vol. I. *The Apostolic Fathers - Justin Martyr - Irenaeus*. Grand Rapids, MI: Wm. B. Eerdmans Publishing Co., 1987.

Rogich, Daniel M., trans. *Saint Gregory Palamas, Treatise on the Spiritual Life*. Minneapolis, MN: Light and Life Publishing Company, 1995.

Rose, Fr. Seraphim. *The Place of the Blessed Augustine in the Orthodox Church*. Platina, CA: St. Herman of Alaska Brotherhood Press.

Schaff, Philip, ed. *Nicene and Post-Nicene Fathers of the Christian Church*. Vol. XI. *St. Chrysostom: Homilies on the Acts of the Apostles and the Epistle to the Romans*. Grand Rapids, MI: Wm. B. Eerdmans Publishing Company, 1980.

———. *NPNF*. Vol. XII. *St. Chrysostom: Homilies on First and Second Corinthians*. Grand Rapids, MI: Wm. B. Eerdmans Publishing Company, 1983.

———. *NPNF*. Vol. XIV, *St. Chrysostom: Homilies on the Gospel of St. John and the Epistle to the Hebrews*. Grand Rapids, MI: Wm. B. Eerdmans Publishing Company, 1989.

Schaff, Philip, and Henry Wace, ed. *NPNF*. Second Series, Vol. IV. *St. Athanasius: Select Works and Letters*. Grand Rapids, MI: Wm. B. Eerdmans Publishing Co., 1980.

———. *NPNF*. Second Series. Vol. VII. *St. Cyril of Jerusalem - St. Gregory Nazianzen*. Grand Rapids, MI: Wm. B. Eerdmans Publishing Company, 1989.

———. *NPNF*. Second Series. Vol. VIII. *St. Basil: Letters and Select Works*. Grand Rapids, MI: Wm. B. Eerdmans Publishing Company, 1983.

Schmemann, Alexander. *The Eucharist*. Crestwood, NY: St. Vladimir's Seminary Press, 1988.

______. *Great Lent.* Crestwood, NY: St. Vladimir's Seminary Press, 1974.

Smith, R. Payne, trans. *Commentary on the Gospel of St. Luke, by Saint. Cyril of Alexandria.* United States of America: Studion Publishers, 1983.

Staniforth, Maxwell, trans. *Early Christian Writings*, New York, NY: Dorset Press, 1986.

Stavropoulos, Christoforos. *Partakers of Divine Nature.* Trans. Stanley Harakas. Minneapolis, MN: Light and Life Publishing Co., 1976.

Toal, M.F., trans and ed. *The Sunday Sermons of the Great Fathers.* 4 vols. Chicago: Henry Regnery Co. London: Longmans, Green, 1957.

Vassiliadis, Nikolaos P. *The Mystery of Death.* Trans. Fr. Peter A. Chamberas. Athens: The Orthodox Brotherhood of Theologians, "The Savior," 1993.

Velimirovic, Bishop Nikolai. *The Prologue From Ochrid, Lives of the Saints and Homilies for Every Day in the Year.* Trans. Mother Maria. Four parts. Birmingham, England: Lazarica Press, 1985.

Ware, Kallistos (Timothy). *The Orthodox Way.* Crestwood, NY: St. Vladimir's Seminary Press, 1990.

Ware, Timothy. *The Orthodox Church.* London and New York, NY: Penguin Books, Inc., 1993.

Winter, David. *Faith Under Fire.* Wheaton, IL: Harold Shaw Publishers, 1977.

Glossary

apostolic succession: the power and authority passed on, in an unbroken chain, from Christ to the Apostles to each succeeding Bishop of the Church through the ages, via the laying on of hands. The Bishops continue the office of the Apostles (see Acts 1:20).

ascesis: The willing struggle through life to grow spiritually, in the image of Christ, to show love and faith, and to prepare for eternal life in God's Kingdom, where holiness is required.

Bishop: From the Greek "episcopos," meaning overseer. A Bishop is the highest rank of the Christian priesthood, the shepherd of the flock of a particular diocese and spiritual father of the priests in that jurisdiction. Only a Bishop can ordain deacons and priests, with the power and authority they have received through Apostolic Succession. The terms Archbishop and Patriarch are administrative titles held by Bishops elected to those offices of broader administrative rights and authority within the Church.

Chrismation: A Sacrament of the Church, through which a person is anointed with Holy Myron (Chrism) and receives indwelling of the Holy Spirit.

Divine Liturgy: The word liturgy (Gr: leitourgia) means "work of the people." Divine Liturgy means the divine work of the people: the worship of God. The Divine Liturgy of the Orthodox Church has its roots in the Mystical Supper of Jesus: He took bread and broke it saying: "Take eat, this is My Body," and passed wine saying: "Drink from...this My Blood" (Mt 26:26-28). From that day on, Christians have gathered regularly to receive His Body and His Blood and to read Scripture, pray and sing hymns of praise and thanksgiving. This ritual evolved into the Divine Liturgy of today.

Eucharist: From the Greek "eucharistia": thanksgiving. This term refers to Holy Communion, the Body and Blood of our Lord Jesus Christ. As Jesus gave thanks to God before offering His Body and His Blood to the Apostles, this word symbolizes Christian thanksgiving for the salvation offered by our Savior through His Crucifixion and Resurrection.

Fathers of the Church: Individuals who labored to defend the Gospel against heresy and misunderstanding. Generally, important Christian writers and teachers from the end of the first century to the end of the eighth, whose understanding in matters of faith is widely trusted within the conscience of the Church. There is particular reverence, within this realm, for writers of the fourth century, especially Sts. Basil, Gregory of Nazianzus, and John Chrysostom. No individual writer or teacher is considered infallible, but the faithful can be guided by the writings of the Fathers where they agree and speak with the Church as a whole.

free will: The gift from God to man and woman as part of being created in His image. This gift grants the freedom to make choices in life, not controlled by God. The most important choice is that of obedience to God

grace: Divine power from God, a bit of His energies, given for purposes of sanctification.

Logos: Our Lord Jesus Christ. (See Word of God.)

Melchizedeck: The mysterious eternal priest who appears suddenly to Abraham in Gen 14:18-20. Melchizedeck was not part of the Hebrew priesthood, which was established with Moses' brother Aaron to offer sacrifices to God for the sins of His people and which came to an end with Christ on the cross as the last living sacrifice, fulfilling Mosaic Law. With no known beginning and no known end, Melchizedeck pointed to the eternal priesthood of Christ (Psalm 110:4).

Mysteries: Vehicles through which God gives of Himself, His grace. (See Sacraments.)

Orthodox Church: The historical Body (of Christ) established by Jesus Christ to carry on His work, unchanged and undiluted since the Apostles, through apostolic succession.

Paraclete: The Holy Spirit.

Priest: From the Greek "presbyter," meaning elder. The clergy of the Church ordained to carry on the eternal priesthood of Christ after the order of Melchizedek (see Gen 14:18, Ps 110:4, Heb 5: 5-10, 7:11-28).

repentance: (Gr: metanoia). The sorrow one feels at having acted or reacted against the will of God. True repentance includes effort to change, so as not to repeat the offence.

Sacraments: more properly called Mysteries (Gr: Mysteria), they are the outer symbols of inner grace received from God. Generally considered seven in number: Baptism, Chrismation (Confirmation), Eucharist, Repentance (Confession), Holy Orders, Holy Matrimony, and Unction (anointing of the sick). Some early Fathers of the Church mention only two, Baptism and Eucharist, but the other five were gradually recognized through the life of the Church. Some theologians maintain that while these seven were clearly accorded the authority of Sacraments, there are other "actions in the Church which also possess a sacramental character, and which are conveniently termed *sacramentals*."[1] In this category are the blessing of water at Epiphany, the service for the burial of the dead, blessing of homes, etc.

Second Coming of Christ: The return of Jesus Christ to earth, as Judge. This event, the timing of which no man knows, will be the end of the world as we know it and the beginning of God's promises. The dead will rise and with transfigured bodies everyone will live eternally, the life for which he has prepared.

Theosis: The spiritual process of deification, growing in union with God, through God's grace and man's willing efforts.

Theotokos: The title, meaning "God-bearer." Given to Mary, who bore in her womb, Jesus Christ, the Son of God, the second person of the Holy Trinity (God, the Son).

Way, the: Those who were Christ's followers in the first days of the Church were said to be in "the Way" (to the Kingdom) (Jn 14:6).

word of God: Holy Scripture.

Word of God: The Son, Logos of God (Jn 1:1-4), who became man to make it possible for man to return to union with God.

---

[1] Timothy Ware, *The Orthodox Church*, p.282.

Index

N

O

P

R